TROPHIES

TAKE FLIGHT

Harcourt

Orlando   Boston   Dallas   Chicago   San Diego

Visit *The Learning Site!*

www.harcourtschool.com

Photo Credits

(t) = top, (b) = bottom, (c) = center, (l) = left, (r) = right, (bkgd) = background.

Page 63(inset), Bob Winsett/Indexstock Imagery; 63, Keith Black/Indexstock Imagery; 64, Kevin Beebe/Indexstock Imagery; 67(inset), Zefa/Indexstock Imagery; 67, Lon Lauber/AlaskaStock; 68, Will Steger/Adventure Photo; 112, Norbert Wu/Tony Stone Images; 114, 115(t), Doug Perrine/Masterfile; 115(c), Stephen Frink/Tony Stone Images; 115(b), Pete Atkinson/Masterfile; (br), Kurt Amsler/Masterfile; 206–207, Ken Kinzie/Harcourt; 207(t), Culver Pictures; 208, The Granger Collection, New York; 210, Stock Montage; 212, Library of Congress; 207, 208, 213 (frames), Photodisc.com; 217, Mark Romesser/Unicorn Stock Photos; 218, H. Schmeiser/Unicorn Stock Photos; 219(t), Alice M. Prescott/Unicorn Stock Photos; 238–239, Darrell Gulin/Tony Stone Images; 239, Peter Cade/Tony Stone Images; 240, Darrell Gulin/Tony Stone Images; 240, 241, Buddy Mays/FPG; 242, Tom Stewart/The Stock Market; 243, Martin Rodgers/Tony Stone Images; 243(inset), Unicorn Stock Photos; 244, Mug Shots/The Stock Market

Illustration Credits

Page 13, Linda Howard Bittner; 93, 189, Joe Boddy; 69, 149, David Brooks; 213, Hector Cuenca; 173, Mike Dammer; 29, 109, Patti Green; 53, 133, 245, Ken Roberts.

For permission to reprint copyrighted material, grateful acknowledgment is made to the following sources:

Alfred A. Knopf Children's Books, a division of Random House, Inc.: Illustrations by Istvan Banyai from *Poems for Children Nowhere Near Old Enough to Vote* by Carl Sandburg. Illustrations copyright © 1999 by Istvan Banyai.

Nickelodeon, a division of Viacom International Inc.: Photographs from *"Zoom"* by Istvan Banyai. Photographs © 2001 by Viacom International Inc.

Viking Penguin, a division of Penguin Putnam Inc.: Cover illustration from *ZOOM* by Istvan Banyai. Copyright © 1995 by Istvan Banyai. Cover illustration from *RE-ZOOM* by Istvan Banyai. Copyright © 1995 by Istvan Banyai. Cover illustration from *REM: Rapid Eye Movement* by Istvan Banyai. Copyright © 1997 by Istvan Banyai.

Copyright © by Harcourt, Inc.

All rights reserved. No part of this publication may be reproduced or transmitted in any form or by any means, electronic or mechanical, including photocopy, recording, or any information storage and retrieval system, without permission in writing from the publisher.

Requests for permission to make copies of any part of the work should be addressed to School Permissions and Copyrights, Harcourt, Inc., 6277 Sea Harbor Drive, Orlando, Florida 32887-6777. Fax: 407-345-2418.

HARCOURT and the Harcourt Logo are trademarks of Harcourt, Inc., registered in the United States of America and/or other jurisdictions.

Printed in the United States of America

ISBN 0-15-325342-8

3 4 5 6 7 8 9 10   039   10 09 08 07 06 05 04 03 02

CONTENTS

5

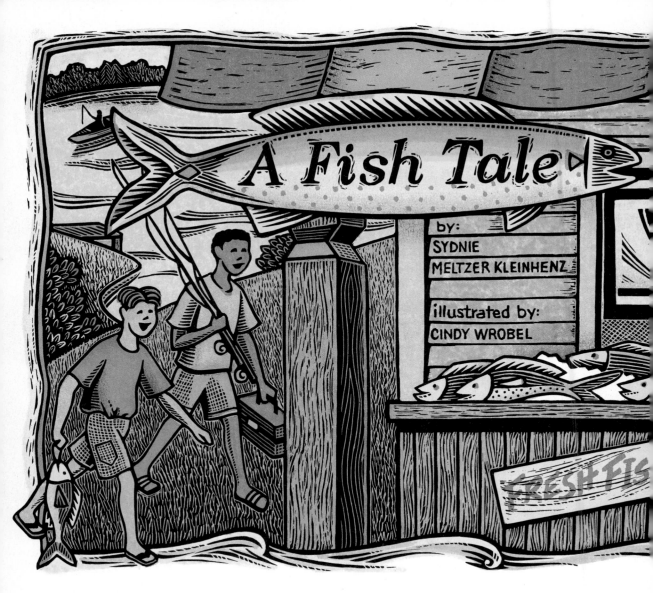

A Fish Tale

by:
SYDNIE
MELTZER KLEINHENZ

illustrated by:
CINDY WROBEL

Ingrid was down by the lakefront one day when she saw Sam and Travis emerge from the brush. Sam swung a tackle box and held their two fishing poles. Travis grasped a line with a fish on it.

Ingrid hovered close by. "Will you let me fish with you?" she asked.

Sam didn't like Ingrid. Her name and the way she spoke were foreign to him. Did she come to Kansas just to bug him?

"No, no, and no, in case you still ask," Sam said with authority.

"I know all things to do," Ingrid said. "When we fished in Finland, my dad said I had a gift for catching big ones."

"Our fishing spot is just for us," Travis said. "We made a vow. No one else must use it."

"Go hug a slug," said Sam.

Five times Ingrid asked to fish with them. Five times she got a no. Then she figured out a plan.

The next day, Ingrid ran with her fishing pole to Al's Fish Shop. She got a big catfish, slipped off to a hiding spot, and strung it on her line. She was stationed on the path when Sam and Travis came back from the lake.

"Incredible!" said Travis. Sam stared with suspicion.

"That's some fish!" said a man.

The man snapped a shot of Ingrid and her fish.

"I'd like to investigate where you got that," Sam said.

"From the lake," said Ingrid. "I will take out the bones at home."

Travis said, "You know how to cut up fish by yourself?"

Ingrid nodded. "Oh, yes!"

"That's a good skill," Travis said. "We could go fishing sometime."

Sam poked him. "What about our vow, Travis?"

Travis shrugged.

Travis and Ingrid went fishing and pulled in some bass. Sam got mad seeing Travis with Ingrid. He tossed rocks into the lake to make a commotion and scare off the fish.

Ingrid and Travis put down their poles. As they got up, Ingrid slipped on some mud. Travis grabbed for her and tripped on a rock. Into the lake they plopped! When they emerged giggling, Sam jumped in with them. They all swam and had fun until they were exhausted. Then they squished off home, dripping wet.

10

The next day, Ingrid was in the *Lakefront News*! "That's you and your catfish!" Sam said to Ingrid. "I'll get you one of these for a souvenir."

Ingrid blushed and bit her lip. "Oh, Sam and Travis! I did a bad thing. I tricked you. I got that fish at Al's shop." She looked ashamed.

Travis said, "We're glad you told us! You're our pal now, Ingrid from Finland." Sam nodded.

"Oh, thank you!" Ingrid said. "Now come with me to *Lakefront News*. I want them to tell my big fish tale!"

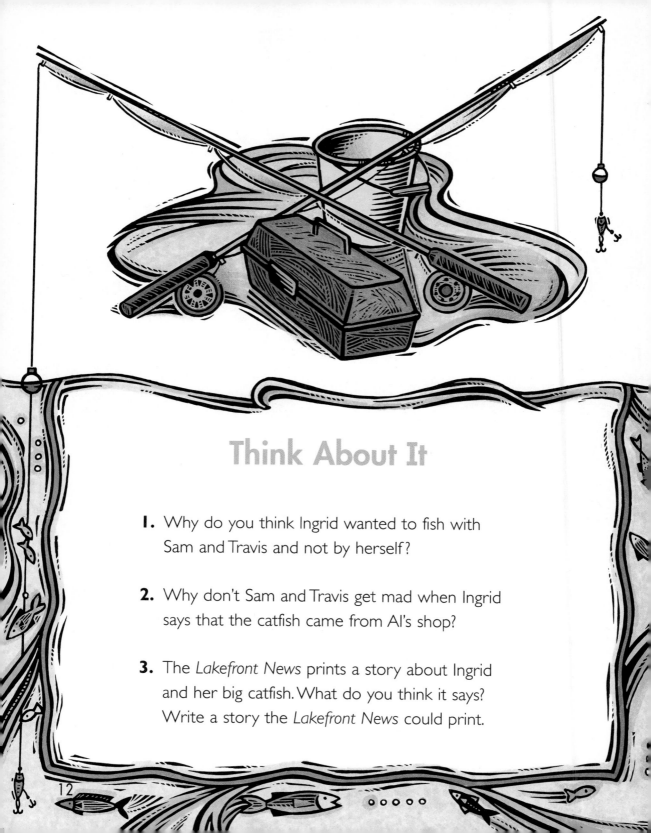

Think About It

1. Why do you think Ingrid wanted to fish with Sam and Travis and not by herself?

2. Why don't Sam and Travis get mad when Ingrid says that the catfish came from Al's shop?

3. The *Lakefront News* prints a story about Ingrid and her big catfish. What do you think it says? Write a story the *Lakefront News* could print.

Something Fishy

That swordfish has quite a jaw! If you'd like to get to know a fish whose *name* is a real jawbreaker, meet the official state fish of Hawaii, the **humuhumunukunukuapuaa.** (Just say hoo-moo-hoo-moo-noo-koo-noo-koo-ah-poo-ah-ah.) It got its Hawaiian name from the way it looks, since the last part of the word means "snout like a pig's." Fortunately, this little fish has a more common name, the triggerfish.

Now that you can say "humuhumunukunukuapuaa," try these tongue twisters:

Do fishes wish to wash dishes, or do
    fishes wish to watch ditches?

Can a perch poach peaches
    for a poached peach pie?

13

THE QUIVER

by Sharon Fear
illustrated by Leslie Wu

Will was lost.

How had he let this happen?

Someone's wagon wheel had broken, so all the wagons had stopped. Without telling Ma or Pa, Will had jumped down and run into the trees, just to look.

That's when he had seen the quiver. Did it belong to a Blackfoot hunter? What an incredible souvenir it would be of this trip!

Will had investigated the creek next, looking for things there. And when he looked up. . . he was lost.

How often had Ma said sternly,
"Don't run off without telling us.
You'll get lost"?

How often had Pa, looking solemn,
said, "If you get lost, you must not panic.
Stay in one spot. We'll find you"?

But Will did panic, running and
falling. The trees and rocks all looked
the same! He found himself weeping—
he just couldn't help it.

A blurry image emerged from the trees. What was it? Will interrupted his sobbing. When the image was less blurry, he could see that it was not an "it," but a "he."

Someone just his size was kicking up leaves and moss. It was clear that he was looking for something.

He looked sad and solemn and about to weep himself. Then he sat down and did just that.

Will realized that he was looking for the quiver. It looked ordinary to Will, but maybe it wasn't ordinary to that boy.

Will composed himself and got up. Hearing Will's tread, the boy jumped up, too, and stepped back. Then, seeing the quiver Will held out, he reached for it.

The boy brushed his hands across his wet cheeks. Then he stepped close and looked at the wet tracks on Will's cheeks. Will had seen his feelings. Now he seemed to see Will's.

The boy looked puzzled when Will got a stick and made lines in the mud. Then he realized what Will was saying with them. *Have you seen a wagon and a team of oxen?*

The boy grinned at Will, gave him a signal to come, and ran off. Will ran to catch up, and they jogged on without speaking. A mile or so on, they broke from the trees and climbed up on some rocks.

Will could see well from here.
No hills or trees interrupted the
flat land, but the deep ruts of
wagon wheels did. To the west,
Will could see the wagons.

He gave a yell and ran down
into the long grass. Then he
looked back and waved.

The boy who had helped him
lifted the quiver one time. Then
he melted back into the trees.

Will's parents did not criticize
him for getting lost. They just
hugged him and let him tell his
incredible tale.

"The quiver seemed to mean
a lot to that boy," said Pa.

"Maybe his ma made it for
him," Will said. "Maybe his pa
gave it to him. I just know he
was very glad to get it back."

"Not as glad as we are to get
you back," said Ma.

She didn't exaggerate—Will
could tell.

Think About It

1. How does Will help the boy he meets? How does that boy help Will?

2. Do you think Will feels bad that the boy has seen him weeping? Why or why not?

3. That night, Will writes in his diary. He writes about what happened and how he felt. Write Will's diary entry.

The Audition

by Susan McCloskey
illustrated by Linda Pierce

Jean looked at the clock on the wall. It was close to ten, when the audition would begin. The hall was filled with kids who hoped to get into the music show. Chad was clutching his trumpet, Jan had set up her drums, and . . . oh, no! There was Aldo with his cello!

This was going to be a problem. Jean also played the cello, and the music show needed just one.

Jean had rehearsed and rehearsed for the audition. She realized that Aldo must also have rehearsed a lot. Jean did not flatter herself that she played well. Still, she hoped she'd win the audition.

Miss Small, who led the music class, walked in. All the kids stopped talking.

"I'll call you up to audition one at a time," Miss Small said. "The rest of you, please be patient and sit still."

"Aldo, you can go first," Miss Small called out.

Aldo sat up in his seat. He nodded to the accompanist, a pianist, and they began to play simultaneously. The notes of a sonata filled the hall.

All of a sudden, Aldo stopped playing, grimaced, and jumped up. The accompaniment came to a halt as well. One of the strings on Aldo's cello had broken!

"Do you have a spare string, Aldo?" asked Miss Small.

"No, ma'am," Aldo said.

Jean smiled to herself. Aldo had just begun his sonata when the string broke. It was as if he hadn't come to the audition at all! Now all she had to do was keep from making blunders in her waltz.

Then Jean stopped to think. If she won the audition, would it be best for the music show?

"Bad luck, Aldo," Miss Small said. "Jean, you're next."

Jean got to her feet. "Miss Small," she said, "if it's all right with you, Aldo can use my cello to finish."

Miss Small smiled. "Thank you, Jean," she said.

Jean smiled, too. Maybe Aldo would win the audition, but she felt that she had done what was best for the music show.

1. Why does Aldo suddenly stop playing the sonata?

2. Why does Jean feel that she has won when Aldo stops playing? Why does she feel that she has done what is right at the end of the story?

3. What do you think happens at the end of the audition? Write down your ideas.

Take Note!

Q: Why do fish make good musicians?
A: They know a lot about scales.

Q: Where do all great composers
write their music?
A: In notebooks.

Q: Why couldn't the singer start his car?
A: He couldn't find the right key.

Q: When the boy skinned his knee, why
did he ask the musicians how old
they were?
A: He needed a band-age.

Q: What's a singer's favorite part of a cake?
A: The I-sing.

Q: What do brass players use when they
brush their teeth?
A: A tuba toothpaste.

Lessons *from* Barbara Jordan

by Kana Riley

illustrated by Stacey Schuett

FROM: Jane Barr
TO: Wilma Downs
DATE: 10/12/00 07:58 PM
SUBJECT: Grandma's Technology!!!

REPLY   SEND   TRASH

Grandma,

I'm so glad you have started to use e-mail. I like sending and getting mail fast! Do you?

Grandma, can you help me? I have to tell my class about Barbara Jordan. Mom said you met her one time. What was she like?

Love, Jane

FROM: Wilma Downs
TO: Jane Barr
DATE: 10/13/00 06:15 PM
SUBJECT: Barbara Jordan

REPLY   SEND   TRASH

Jane,

I did meet Barbara Jordan. She was making a speech. That speech inspired me! I was glad to meet a smart woman with such dignity and confidence.

Did your mom tell you about Ms. Jordan's career?
Love, Grandma
P.S. How far we have come! Correspondence was not this fast when I was ten. This e-mail technology is lots of fun!

FROM: Jane Barr
TO: Wilma Downs
DATE: 10/13/00 08:15 PM
SUBJECT: Barbara Jordan's Career

REPLY   SEND   TRASH

Grandma,
      Mom said that Ms. Jordan sat in Congress.
What else did she do?
Love, Jane

FROM: Wilma Downs
TO: Jane Barr
DATE: 10/14/00 02:01 PM
SUBJECT: Rep. Jordan

REPLY SEND TRASH

Jane,

Barbara Jordan got her start in the Texas Senate. There were few African Americans in the Senate then, but no one ridiculed her.

Ms. Jordan's peers admired her sense of dignity. They had confidence in her work and counseled her to run for the U.S. Congress. She did so, and Texans elected her to Congress three times.

Then Ms. Jordan became ill and came home to Texas. When she got well, she started a new career. She wanted to teach, and she was very good at it.
Love, Grandma

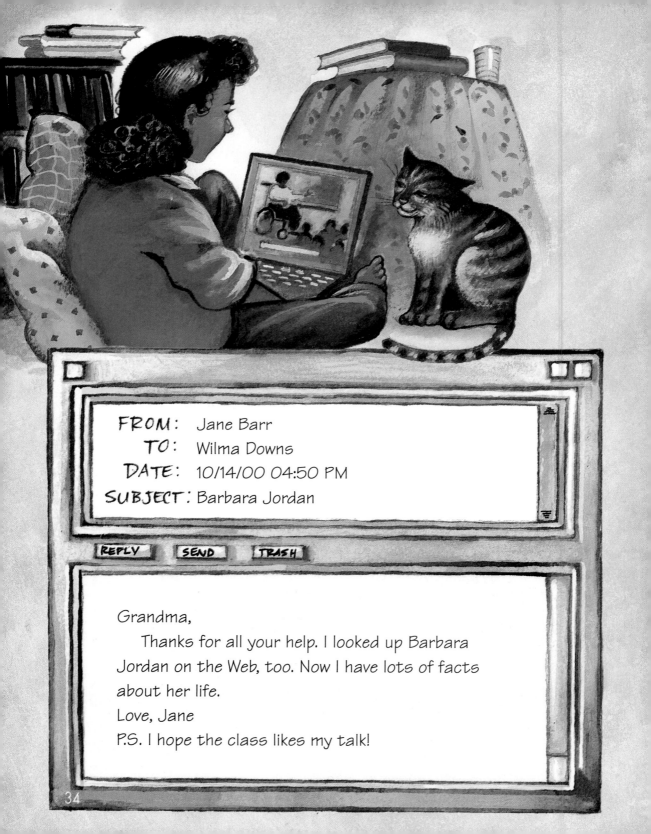

FROM: Jane Barr
TO: Wilma Downs
DATE: 10/14/00 04:50 PM
SUBJECT: Barbara Jordan

REPLY   SEND   TRASH

Grandma,
    Thanks for all your help. I looked up Barbara Jordan on the Web, too. Now I have lots of facts about her life.
Love, Jane
P.S. I hope the class likes my talk!

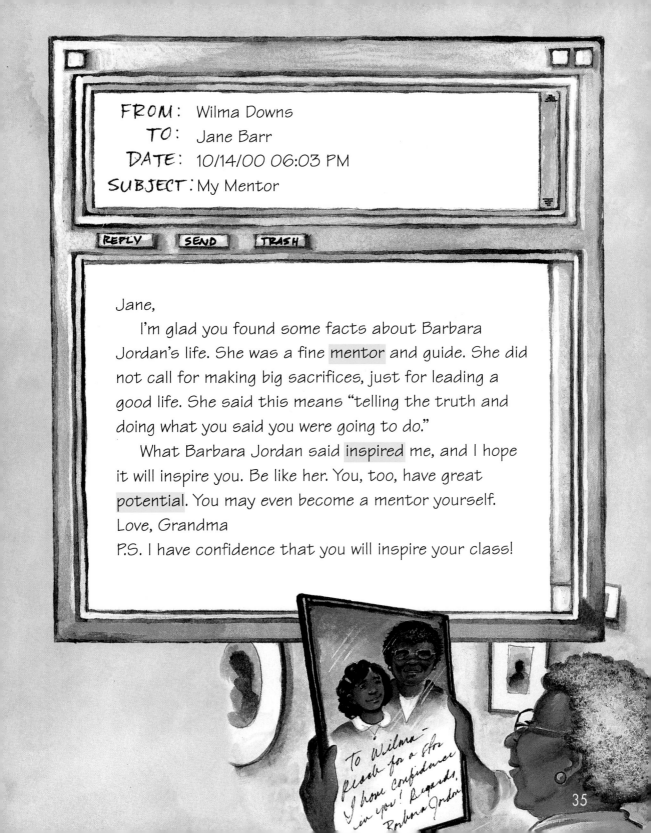

FROM: Wilma Downs
TO: Jane Barr
DATE: 10/14/00 06:03 PM
SUBJECT: My Mentor

REPLY   SEND   TRASH

Jane,

I'm glad you found some facts about Barbara Jordan's life. She was a fine mentor and guide. She did not call for making big sacrifices, just for leading a good life. She said this means "telling the truth and doing what you said you were going to do."

What Barbara Jordan said inspired me, and I hope it will inspire you. Be like her. You, too, have great potential. You may even become a mentor yourself.

Love, Grandma

P.S. I have confidence that you will inspire your class!

To Wilma—
Reach for a star.
I have confidence
in you! Regards,
Barbara Jordan

FROM: Jane Barr
TO: Wilma Downs
DATE: 10/16/00 07:52 PM
SUBJECT: TA-DA!!!

REPLY   SEND   TRASH

Grandma,
    I got an A+ for my report on Barbara Jordan!
The class liked my talk a lot. Now they want to
hear what else she did for humanity. Will you come
to class and tell us all about her?
Love, Jane

To Wilma -
Reach for a star
I have confidence
in you! Regards,
Barbara Jordan

Think About It

1. Why does Jane ask her grandma about Barbara Jordan? Why does she also look up Barbara Jordan on the Web?

2. Why do you think Barbara Jordan made a good teacher?

3. Jane's grandma comes to class and talks about Barbara Jordan. After that visit, Jane sends another e-mail to thank her grandma. Write the e-mail Jane sends.

PAINTING
My Homeland

by Deborah Akers • illustrated by Mark Schroder

Diego Rivera was born in Mexico in 1886. He painted many murals in his country. He became one of Mexico's greatest artists.

Diego, Pablo, and Ren walked down to the end of the dock.

"It's too bad you must leave this fine land, Diego," said Pablo. "You have my condolences."

Ren said, "Why are you going back home, when you have so much here in Italy?"

Diego Rivera stared at the bay. "I am urgently needed in Mexico," he said. "I must paint the story of my homeland."

"Ha! Our homeland," Pablo scoffed in a mocking tone. "They do not care for art there. They care for farms and cattle. How will you get paid?"

Diego did not say a word. Pablo and Ren gave up. They could see the determination in his eyes. There was not a thing they could say to detain him.

Diego sailed for Mexico the next day.

Time passed. Diego had been back in Mexico for nine years.

Two men walked into a big hall. They made an odd pair. One man was small and frail. Next to him was Diego, with his big frame and wild hair. Diego had become known for creating art on walls.

The wide, white walls called urgently to him. Diego walked up and down, creating as he stared at them.

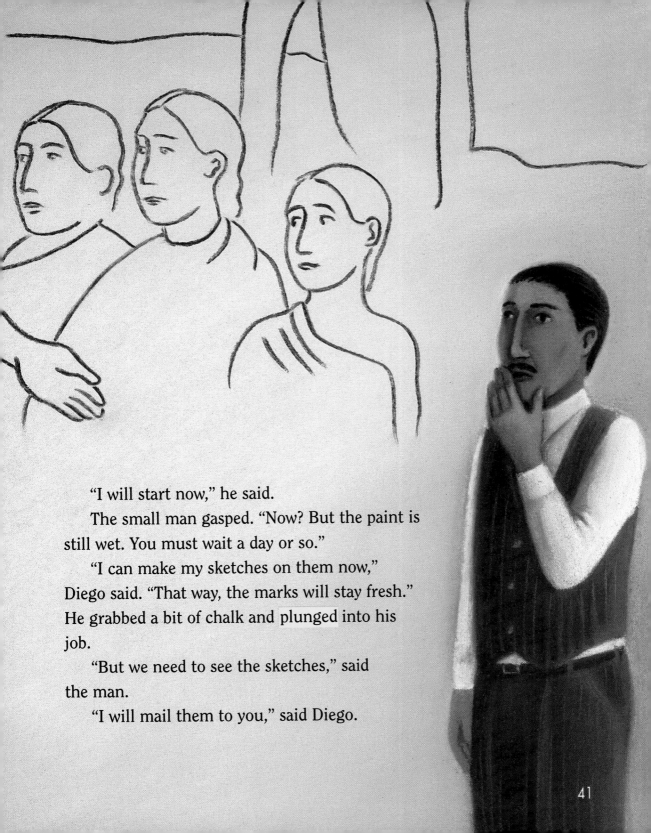

"I will start now," he said.

The small man gasped. "Now? But the paint is still wet. You must wait a day or so."

"I can make my sketches on them now," Diego said. "That way, the marks will stay fresh." He grabbed a bit of chalk and plunged into his job.

"But we need to see the sketches," said the man.

"I will mail them to you," said Diego.

41

Diego stayed at the hall for days at a time. He painted jungle ravines filled with vines. He painted old stone temples. He painted people bending to plant their land.

Diego painted with courage. His art spoke of the revolution in his land. He painted widows, sad from the loss of their husbands. But his painting also spoke of hopes and dreams.

Diego wanted his art to speak in a genuine way of the past. He also wanted people to see what was to come for their land.

No one had been let into the hall. Diego did not want to be detained from his work by talk. Now he invited Pablo to come and see his painting. Pablo stared and stared at the walls.

"This is a genuine work of art," he said to Diego. "You have real courage!"

At last the day came to display the art on the walls. Some who saw it were shocked.

"This is not art!" they scoffed. "It is just the jungle and old temples and farms."

Some did not want Diego to get paid. But one old widow came up and grasped his hand.

"Thank you for painting the story of our land," she said.

Diego smiled at her. His work for his homeland had not been in vain!

Think About It

1. What things did Diego put into his paintings?

2. Why do you think the widow liked Diego's paintings so much?

3. What advice do you think Diego might give to a young painter? Write your ideas.

The Pirate Hero

by David Lopez
illustrated by Liz Sayles

When Roberto Clemente first came to the Pittsburgh Pirates in 1955, he made a vow—he promised himself that he would play hard for the team.

In 1971, the Pirates were playing a set of games with the Baltimore Orioles. One of these teams would be the best team in baseball.

Some people said the Pirates couldn't beat the ace lineup of the Orioles. To Clemente, that was an error. His team was going to win!

The Pirates went to Baltimore for the first two games. The billboard at the ballpark read "Home of the Orioles." Filled with confidence, the home team won game 1. Pirates fans looked solemn when their team lost game 2 as well.

For the next game, the team was glad to be back in Pittsburgh. There the billboard greeted the Pirates, and fans hoped the team could make a comeback.

An Oriole error helped the Pirates win game 3. That was fine, but it wasn't time for them to boast yet—they had to keep winning!

Led by the man with the 21 on his uniform, the Pirates won games 4 and 5.

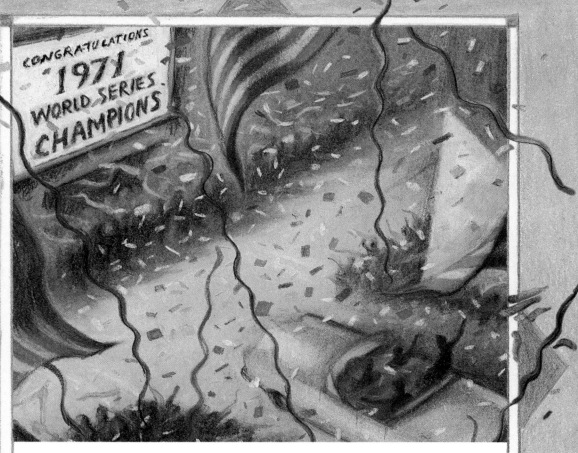

Congratulations
1971
WORLD SERIES
CHAMPIONS

Now the games went back to Baltimore, and people there said the home team would win again.

In five games, Clemente had gotten at least one hit a game. In game 6, he got two hits—one of them a home run. But the Orioles still won the game.

Clemente got one hit in game 7. It was a home run, and this time the Pirates won the game.

The games were over, and the Pirates were the best team in baseball for 1971! Clemente was a hero to Pittsburgh fans.

Clemente was a star to all baseball fans, and they praised his fine playing. He was glad to have the praise, but he didn't boast. He had just kept his promise to play hard.

Roberto Clemente was a hero in and out of baseball. When he wasn't helping his team, he was helping people in need.

For example, Clemente met someone who needed to get artificial legs. Clemente gave some of the money himself. Then he helped raise the rest of it.

In 1972, Roberto Clemente lost his life. It happened when he was helping people. Clemente was taking help to some people who needed it. The plane crashed after take-off—the control tower did not see it going down.

The people of Pittsburgh dedicated a statue to Clemente. The artist sculpted him in his uniform with the number 21 on it. Fans can visit the statue and dream that Roberto Clemente is still playing for the Pirates.

Think About It

1. How did Roberto Clemente help the Pittsburgh Pirates? How did he help other people?

2. Why do you think Clemente didn't boast? How do you think that made the fans feel about him?

3. Think about Roberto Clemente. Make a web with words that tell what he did. Then write a paragraph describing Roberto Clemente.

What Do You Call . . . ?

a disappointed batter on a baseball team | bitter hitter

a player with a big new contract | richer pitcher

a heavy stick for hitting the ball | fat bat

the person who gives paychecks to team members | player payer

bread browned in the oven | roast toast

a happy father | glad dad

a jacket to be worn on a ship | boat coat

a skimpy meal | thinner dinner

53

The Rain and the Snow

by Meish Goldish

illustrated by Karen A. Jerome

One day, the rain and the snow came out at the same time.

"Go home, Snow," said Rain. "No one needs you."

Snow asked, "Who says so, Rain? It is you that no one needs."

"That is not so!" Rain assured Snow. "People do need me. Now, go home! I am growing impatient with you!"

54

Rain and Snow kept up their
bellowing. All the while, the sun hovered
over them. Sun was the eldest of the three.

Rain said to Snow, "Let us ask Sun. She
has much wisdom. Let Sun say which of
us is needed and which is not."

"That is fine with me," said Snow.

Snow followed Rain. They plodded
up and up on a long, slow journey.

At last the two reached the glowing sun.

Sun beamed at them. "Rain! Snow! I am so glad to see you."

Rain said, "Sun, we have entrusted you with settling a problem for us. I claim that no one needs Snow."

"I claim that no one needs Rain," Snow said.

At first Sun did not say a thing. She was slow to take sides.

"I cannot tell from what you say," Sun explained. "I must know what you can do. The two of you must show me what you do for people. Then I can say who is needed and who is not."

"That is fine," Rain said. "I will show you what I do."

He sent down a bountiful flow of rain. It soaked the land. It made the grass and the willow trees grow.

"There, Sun!" Rain crowed. "That shows the work I do! When rain is scarce, people complain. Their wheat and oats do not grow!"

Sun said, "I admire your diligence, Rain. Now, I know Snow must be impatient. Let's let her show the work she does."

Snow sent down hundreds of snowflakes. They were blown all over. In no time, the land was all white. People on the road could not finish their journey.

Children and grown-ups looked out their windows. Then they ran outside. They laughed as they made animal shapes in the snow. They had fun throwing snowballs.

"Do you see that, Sun?" crowed Snow. "People like to play in the snow. They complain when it is scarce."

Rain and Snow looked up at Sun. They waited for her to speak her wisdom.

"I am the eldest," said Sun. "Let me show you the work I do."

Sun glowed at the rain, which stopped flowing. In its place was a fine rainbow.

Then Sun glowed at the snow, which melted. The white land went back to being green.

"Speak little and do a lot," said Sun. "People need each of you. Go out and do what you can for them. That is your destiny."

Think About It

1. How does Sun settle the quarrel between Rain and Snow?

2. How do you think Sun feels about the quarrel?

3. What do you think Rain and Snow will say to each other the next time they meet? Write the conversation.

RACE FOR LIFE ON THE IDITAROD TRAIL

by Caren B. Stelson

❄ It is 1925 in Nome, Alaska. The wind is blowing, and the snow is deep, but Dr. Welch is not thinking of that. He is thinking of two children who are very ill with diphtheria (dif•THEER•ee•uh). Diphtheria is a disease that people can catch from those who have it. It is a disease that kills—and kills fast.

Dr. Welch is afraid for the two children. He is also afraid for Nome. Unless he can get the right medicine, all of Nome may be wiped out. The medicine Dr. Welch needs is 1,000 miles away in Anchorage. The obstacles to transporting it are incredible. Boats and planes are of no use in this wind and snow. Nome will have to save itself in this emergency. But how?

All of Nome may be wiped out.

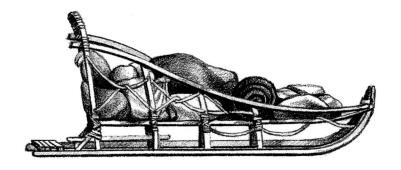

❄ At a meeting, Dr. Welch explains the emergency. A plan is made to transport the medicine to Nome from the medical headquarters in Anchorage. Dogsledding champions—20 in all—will bring it. They and their huskies will follow the mail route, the Iditarod Trail.

Some people think it will take two weeks to sled this route, but these mushers are champions. They say they can do it in less than a week. They plan to sled without stopping.

A train takes the medicine to Nenana, 674 miles from Nome, where the trail begins. There Bill Shannon straps the box to his sled and yells "Mush!" to his huskies. The race to save Nome is on.

Edgar Kalland is waiting 50 miles away. When Shannon arrives, Kalland puts the box on his sled and takes off. Day after day, the medicine travels nonstop, passing from one musher to the next.

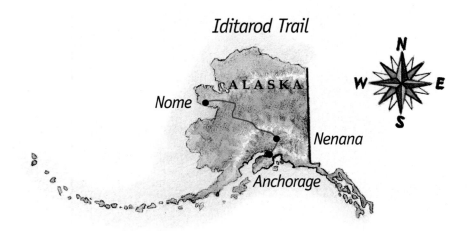

Iditarod Trail

❄ Then a snowstorm hits. The huskies can't keep pace. They step out of their positions and tangle their lines. The mushers must unknot the lines with freezing hands. There are no extra dog handlers along to help—not in this race. The mushers must do their best alone. They must overcome such obstacles and keep going. They dare not stop.

Almost five days have passed. Musher Gunnar Kaasen has the medicine on his sled. Kaasen and his huskies have covered 50 freezing miles, but Nome is still 3 miles away. Will they make it?

In the early morning darkness, Dr. Welch hears a rap at his door. There stands Gunnar Kaasen with a bundle. He unknots the string and hands Dr. Welch a box. The race for life has been won. The people of Nome are saved.

Think About It

1. Why did the medicine have to get to Nome fast? Why was the medicine taken on dogsleds?

2. Why do you think the dogsledding champions offered to help take the medicine to Nome?

3. After he rests, Gunnar Kaasen tells his friends about his part of the trip to Nome. What do you think he says? Write your ideas.

Gunnar Kaasen and his dogs have saved Nome.

On the Trail

Sentences like these are often called Tom Swifties.

"Huskies are great at pulling sleds,"
    Tom said doggedly.

"Please tell me which way is north,"
    Tom said directly.

"I can barely see through this
    blizzard," Tom said stormily.

"I think it's time to stop," Tom
    said haltingly.

"There's ice all over the cabin walls and floor," Tom said coldly.

"Have some more cake," Tom said sweetly.

"One of us should stand watch at
    the door tonight," Tom said
    guardedly.

Now make up
some of your
own!

FISHING FOR FOUR

by Celeste Albright   illustrated by Daniel Powers

"Get on board, kids."

Dad helped the three of us into our rowboat to go out to our big boat. Suze and I sat on the board seat across the back. Elinore, who is just four, sat on the floor of the boat. Dad picked up the oars. Pull, glide. Pull, glide. The rhythm of the oars bore us over the waves.

Our dad fishes for crabs. When the store has no bait
for his traps, we help him catch some. Fishing isn't a
chore to the four of us. We like it.

"I'm going to catch more fish than you!" Suze said
pointedly. She and I like to compete.

The boat emitted a roar as it started up. Then it
settled to a chug-chug rhythm.

Dad made sure our life jackets were buckled. Little Elinore wore her harness over her life jacket's bulk. A line connects the front of it to the boat and keeps her from falling overboard. Suze and I are gratified that we are too big to need harnesses now.

Dad steered the boat far offshore. Then he disengaged the motor. It emitted a snort and was still.

"How much bait do you need for tomorrow?" I asked.

Dad calculated. "If we can fill four bushel baskets, that will do it."

I dropped my line overboard. So did Suze and Elinore. We were fishing for bottom fish.

For a time, all was still. Elinore ignored her line. She was exploring a seashell inside a trap.

"Got one!" Suze yelled. Before you could blink, a big fish was flopping on the deck.

Then there was a tug on my line. I pulled it in fast. One more wiggling fish had retired from swimming!

The sleek fish resembled a little man with long whiskers. When its lips parted, I could see small white teeth. I felt bad for the poor, innocent thing. It was going to end up in a crab trap, but I had to help my dad.

Suze and I were still competing. Suze was keeping score. She calculated on her fingers. "I have four more than you!" she crowed.

I got three big ones. I needed two more to win. Dad looked gratified that our baskets were filling up.

"Time to go home," he said. It was starting to get dark.

I felt a tug. "Wait!" I said. "I've got one more."

Dad grabbed for the net. "Make that two more!" he said.

"I'm the winner!" I yelled.

"Nope," Suze said. "Look at that!" We had forgotten Elinore. Fish overflowed her basket and poured onto the deck. She wore a big, innocent grin. A bunch of fish had met their match, and so had Suze and I.

Dad rowed us to shore. Elinore fell asleep, but Suze and I watched the sun set over the sea we adore.

Think About It

1. Why does the family go out fishing? How do the three girls feel about fishing?

2. How do you think the other girls feel about Elinore getting the most fish? Why do you think that?

3. What do you think the three girls will talk about the next time they go fishing with their dad? Write what they might say.

Raindrop in the Sun

by Deborah Akers   **illustrated by Miles Hyman**

Moro said Lani couldn't go with the men to gather abalones.

"Lani, you are a girl. How could you paddle a canoe? Also, these shells are very hard to get off a rock. You must be strong for this work."

Moro gave Lani a fierce look. Then he strode off to the canoes. There was no more to be said.

Lani was sad. She was also mad.

"I *am* strong. I could paddle a canoe. I could get the abalones off the rocks, too."

People from the tribe gathered on the shore. Lani and her mother watched the canoes set out. Lani looked forlorn.

Before Kalo, Lani's brother, got in his canoe, he gave her a hug. "It's not fair, is it?"

"No! I could help you bring home more meat," Lani said.

"Do you think you could?" Kalo gave his sister a hard look. Then he whispered, "Meet me over at the entrance to the cove. I will hide you in my canoe."

Lani looked up at her mother, who gave her a slow smile. Then she nodded for Lani to go. Lani turned and ran for the cove. She got to the entrance before the canoes did.

When Kalo pulled up, Lani leaped into his canoe. She curled up on the bottom so no one could see her.

Kalo paddled hard. Then he floated the canoe into a rock shelter.

"We need to look low on the rocks for big shells. The big ones will have more meat," he said.

They came to some rocks with lots of seals perched on them. The seals sat in their lair and gorged on fish. They sunned themselves and admired their sleek coats. One big fellow, vainer than the rest, licked his fur all over.

Kalo and Lani smiled at each other and paddled on. Past the seals' lair, they discovered rocks with big abalones stuck to them. They lost no time in getting to work.

Kalo would grab a shell, and Lani would scrape it off with the paddle. Together they made a good team. They were quick workers, and before long they had a big load.

"We should be getting home now," said Kalo. "The waves are getting big."

In no time a fierce storm was upon them. They could see the other canoes coming their way. Then a gigantic wave flipped all those canoes over!

Kalo and Lani had to get to the men in the water. They both grabbed paddles, but they couldn't get up any speed.

"Throw the abalones over the side!" yelled Kalo. "They're making us too slow!"

Lani pitched all the shells but one. When they got to the canoes, Lani reached out with her paddle. She turned each one right side up. Kalo pulled Moro from the water, and the two of them helped the other men. Then they all paddled for shelter.

At last they were safe on shore. Mama and the others ran out to meet them.

Lani held out the shell she had saved. "This shell is for you, Mama. It's not much, but you can make beads from the lining."

The abalone shell was lined with mother-of-pearl. Deep inside the meat, there was something more. It was something not one of them had ever seen—an abalone pearl. Its colors shone like a raindrop in the sun.

Moro strode forward and spoke. He said the pearl was a trophy for their hero, Lani. Mama was overcome when Moro talked of how Lani and Kalo had saved the men. She was so glad to have her strong, brave girl safe at home again.

84

Think About It

1. Why does Moro say Lani can't go with the men to gather abalones?

2. Why do you think Kalo takes his sister along to gather abalones? How do you think he feels when the fierce storm comes up?

3. The next time the men go out to gather abalones, Lani and some other girls ask to go along. Write what you think they say and what the men tell them.

The Gift of the Manatee

by Kathryn Corbett • illustrated by Barbara Hranilovich

"Happy birthday!" Grandpa said. "Go on, open your gift!"

Jason opened the box. Inside lay a model of an odd-looking animal.

Jason pondered it and asked, "What is it, Grandpa? A walrus?"

"It's a manatee," Grandpa told him. "Some call it a sea cow."

"I've never seen a manatee," Jason said. "Where do they live?"

"They live in warm, shallow rivers and bays. In fact, some live right here in Florida," Grandpa replied. "However, they may not live here much longer."

"Why, Grandpa?" Jason asked. "Are they getting ready to migrate?"

"They do migrate," Grandpa said, "but only from the bays to the warmer rivers in winter."

"If they don't stay in Florida," Jason asked, "where will they live?"

"Nowhere at all, Jason. Only a small number remain now. Someday they may all have vanished."

Jason turned the little manatee over in his hands. "That's sad, Grandpa. Why are there not many left? Will you tell me about the manatees?"

"I'll be glad to," Grandpa said, and he began the tale of the manatees.

"Believe it or not, manatees were land animals eons ago. They scurried about with other mammals of that time. Then, perhaps to escape an enemy or find a better food supply, they left the land. They became water mammals."

"Like whales," Jason said.

"That's right," Grandpa said. "In the water they changed and survived."

"How did the manatees change?" Jason asked.

"Over time, their front legs became flippers. Their hind legs vanished. Their tails became flat paddles to help them swim.

"These large animals need an abundance of plants to feed on. In fact, they help keep the plenitude of weeds from choking some of the state's waterways. Manatees live on both sides of the Florida peninsula. Some of them gather in the shallow waters of the Everglades."

"Do manatees live anywhere else?" Jason asked.

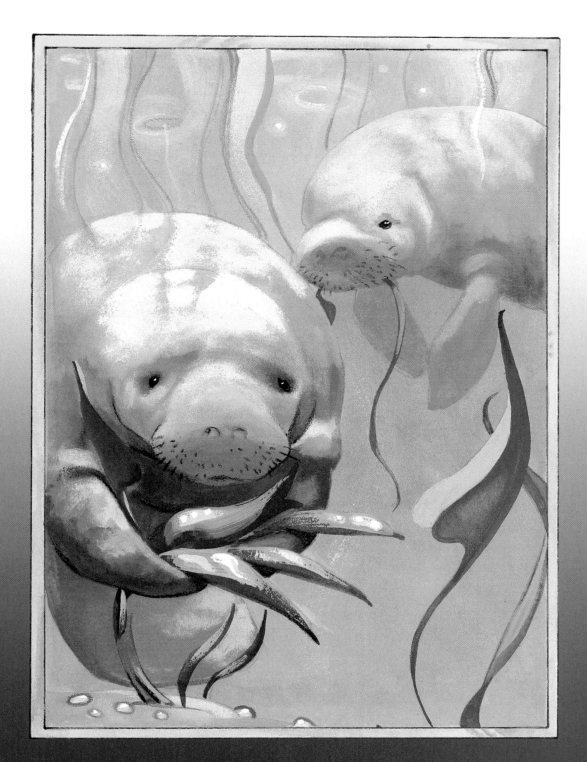

"Yes, but only in warm waters," Grandpa told him. "They can be found in West Africa, along the Amazon River, and in the Caribbean Sea."

Jason asked, "If the manatees have survived so long, why are they dying out now?"

Grandpa replied, "People are their enemy, Jason. Speeding boaters run over them. Their habitats are drained to make more land for homes and shopping malls. Once there were multitudes of manatees. Now they're nearly all gone. It may be too late to save them."

"No!" Jason shouted. "It's not too late to save the ones that remain. I hope that in my lifetime, Florida will see a new abundance of manatees."

He jumped to his feet. "Come on, Grandpa! We're going to the library. I have a lot of reading to do about manatees. Then I'm going to get on the Web. If I find a manatee club, I'll become a member. If I don't, I'll start one."

Grandpa winked. "I'll be in it!"

Jason held up his model. "Thanks for the gift of the manatee!" he said.

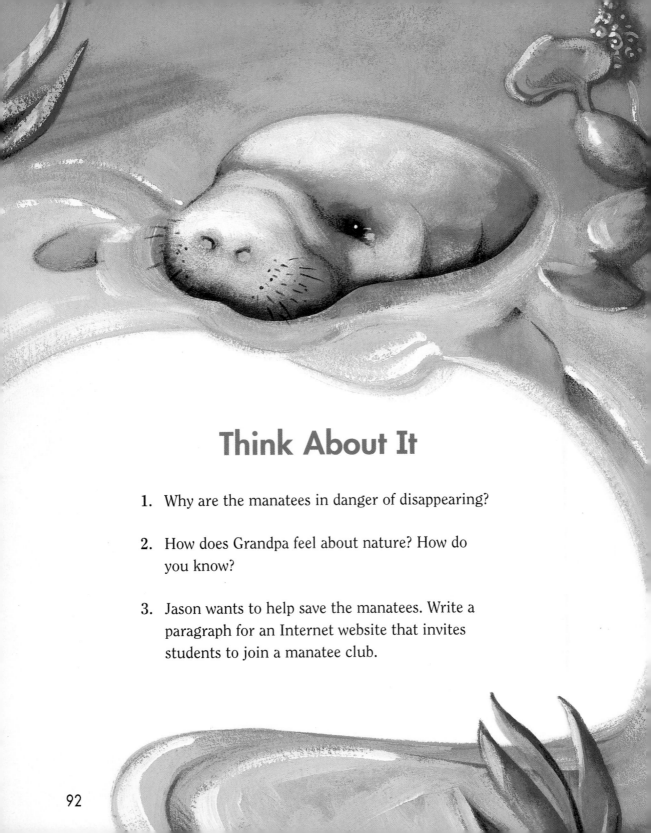

Think About It

1. Why are the manatees in danger of disappearing?

2. How does Grandpa feel about nature? How do you know?

3. Jason wants to help save the manatees. Write a paragraph for an Internet website that invites students to join a manatee club.

In the News

WILDLIFE GROUP REQUESTS FUNDS TO BUY SKUNKS

Critics say proposal stinks

BILL PASSED TO STOP TRAPPING OF ALLIGATORS

New law will have more bite

WEASEL-LIKE ANIMALS DISAPPEAR FROM WILDLIFE PARK

Officials promise to ferret out thieves

RESEARCHERS ARE PUZZLED ABOUT GLOWING INSECTS

Questions about fireflies bug scientists

SHOULD BEAVERS BE REMOVED FROM LOCAL CREEK?

"Naw!" say the animals' fans

FLOWERS AFTER THE FLAMES

by Kana Riley   illustrated by Ed Young

The spring of 1988 started out like any other at Yellowstone National Park. Geysers spouted. Hot springs steamed. Animals roamed the forests, eating the grasses.

Then the days turned warm. Little rain fell, and the grasses turned brown. Yellowstone became as dry as tinder.

In June fires broke out. No one was surprised—fires happened every year. It was park policy to let them burn until rain showers ended them. This year, however, there were no rain showers.

Summer went by with no rain in the forecast. Fierce winds made the fires veer this way and that. Acre after acre burned.

The forest canopy went up in flames. Red-hot embers fell to the ground and started more fires. The entire region was threatened.

In late summer, fire workers dumped water and chemicals from planes. They needed to stop the fires to defend the rest of the park from the flames. By this time, however, it was too late for the water and the chemicals to help.

At last, in September, snow and rain were forecast. When they fell, they damped down the fires. The flames dwindled and finally went out.

The fires had not threatened the geysers or harmed the hot springs at Yellowstone. However, almost half of the park was blackened. It would take a long time to look the same again.

As the land renewed itself, surprising changes happened. Animals and plants found new ways to survive.

The animals' first need was for food. In the beginning the elk licked the ash for minerals. Then, in just two or three days, grass began to spring up. The elk nibbled it eagerly.

The heat of the fires had popped open the cones of tall pine trees. The seeds that spilled onto the ground fed birds and small animals.

Through the winter the land did not offer a lot to eat. Many animals, however, found enough to keep alive.

Then spring came again, and the snow melted. With each warming day, new life returned to the region.

Water trickled down into the scorched, black ground. There it soaked the hidden seeds, helping them sprout.

Spring breezes scattered seeds from plants and trees that had not burned. They, too, began to grow.

Before long, bison gathered to feed on sweet grasses. Brown bears gobbled berries from new green bushes.

Where trees used to shade the ground, the sun now shone. Flowers burst open everywhere. Acres of yellow and pink blossoms filled the new grasslands.

The sounds of birds filled the blackened forest. Woodpeckers pounded holes in burned trees to look for insects. Other birds sang from charred treetops to defend their new territories.

On the forest floor, new little pine trees sprouted. In 40 more years, they would form another forest of tall pines.

The fires had done their job. Their flames had made way for renewed life at Yellowstone.

Think About It

1. What good came of the forest fires in Yellowstone?

2. How do you think the people around Yellowstone felt about the fires in the summer of 1988?

3. You visit Yellowstone Park the summer after the forest fires and send a postcard to a friend. Write what you might tell your friend.

THE KRAKATOA WAVE

BY LEE CHANG   ILLUSTRATED BY KEITH WARD

Krakatoa was a towering volcano that rose from the sea floor near the Indian Ocean. It had three cones, the tallest one more than 2,600 feet high.

The volcano's tip formed a beautiful island. The island of Krakatoa got plenty of sunshine and rain, so its forests were thick and green. Birds sang in the tall trees, and it was a peaceful place.

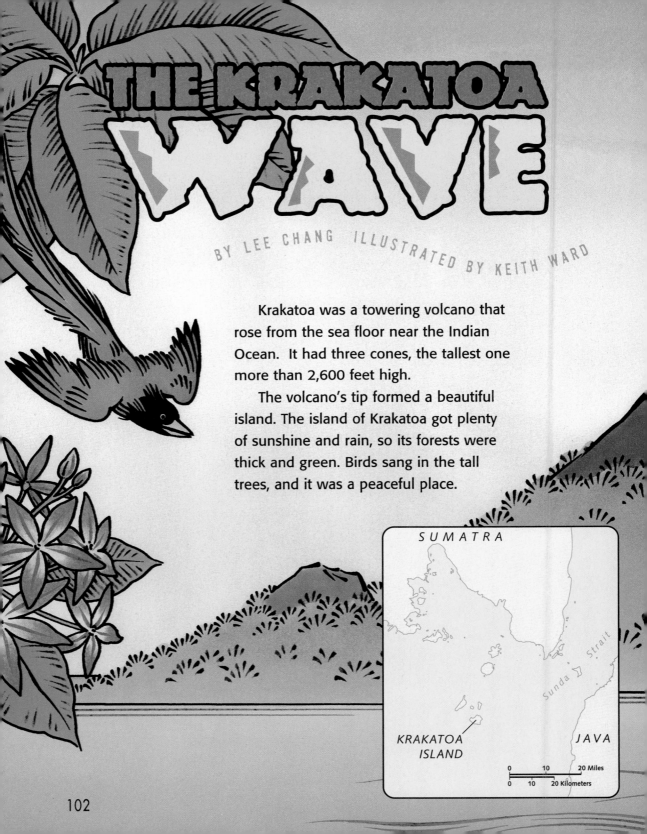

SUMATRA

Sunda Strait

KRAKATOA ISLAND

JAVA

0   10   20 Miles
0   10   20 Kilometers

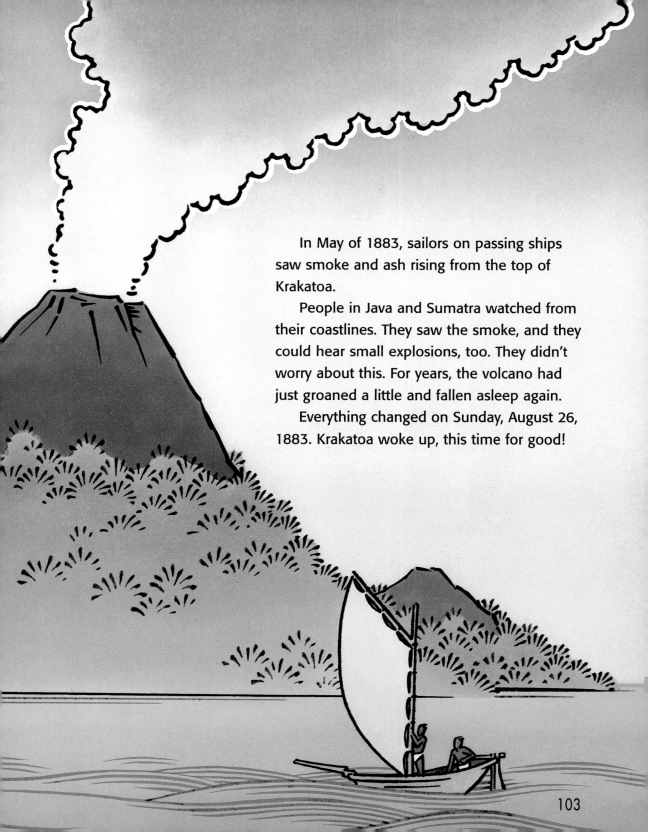

In May of 1883, sailors on passing ships saw smoke and ash rising from the top of Krakatoa.

People in Java and Sumatra watched from their coastlines. They saw the smoke, and they could hear small explosions, too. They didn't worry about this. For years, the volcano had just groaned a little and fallen asleep again.

Everything changed on Sunday, August 26, 1883. Krakatoa woke up, this time for good!

A fierce explosion rocked the island, and the ground began to shake with earthquakes. Steam, smoke, and hot ash shot 17 miles into the sky! The ash formed such dark clouds that daytime turned to night.

The ocean began to rise and fall in a crazy way, smashing the boats in the inlet.

Then a tall wave rushed from the island to the shores of Sumatra and Java. Earthquakes underwater had generated a tsunami!

The tsunami wasn't like an ordinary high wave. It didn't come from the tidal bulge made by the gravitational pull of the moon. It was powered by the energy of the earthquakes started by the explosion.

The tsunami hit the coastlines hard. Frantic people ran from its path. They rushed to high ground where they might find shelter. They wished the volcano would go back to sleep, but the red glow over Krakatoa got brighter and brighter.

The next morning, great explosions began to pound the air. Krakatoa was blowing apart! The biggest blast could be heard 2,500 miles away. Later, it was said to be the loudest sound ever made on Earth.

Without warning, a new tsunami rushed over the ocean with amazing speed. The wave got bigger and bigger as it crossed the shallow waters near the coastlines. Now it was a monster wave, more than 120 feet high!

The tsunami hit the shores of Java and Sumatra with staggering might. It wiped out 165 towns. More than 36,000 people died. Not a house, not a tree, not a person was left.

The mighty wave went far around the world. It traveled 3,800 miles across the ocean in just 12 hours. (A ship would have taken 12 days!)

More than 100 years have passed, and other tsunamis have come and gone. There will be more in the years to come, but Krakatoa's wave will never be forgotten.

Think About It

1. What is a tsunami? What happened when the Krakatoa tsunami hit Java and Sumatra?

2. Why do you think Krakatoa's wave will not be forgotten?

3. Think about how Krakatoa's island looked before and after the volcano woke up. Write two lists of words and word groups to describe the island. Use your lists to write a paragraph about the island before and after Krakatoa exploded.

Making Waves

If you can say "tsunami," you can say two Japanese words. *Tsunami* comes from the Japanese words for *port (tsu)* and *waves (nami).*

When two tsunamis meet, how could they show they're friendly?
    Wave.

What did one mountain say to the other mountain when they met?
    "High!"

What did the volcano say just before it erupted?
    "I'd just lava good earthquake."

What did the mighty volcano say to the smaller volcano?
    "Your cone is all right, but mine is crater."

How did the sailors know what was on the volcanic island?
    They had been to sea.

Why did the band keep playing during the earthquake?
    It really rocked.

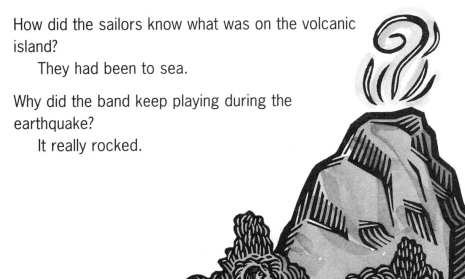

Gardens of the Sea:
Coral Reefs

by Caren B. Stelson   illustrated by James Noel Smith

If you could look down from space, you would see why Earth is called the blue planet. As the blue parts of a globe show, more than two-thirds of Earth is water.

The world's oceans are teeming with life, with the warmest waters being the richest. Here vast numbers of sea animals make their homes. Here, too, the beautiful coral reefs grow. They are the gardens of the sea.

Coral reefs are found in oceans around the world, but only in the warmest waters. For most corals, the water must be between 75 and 85 degrees—almost like bathwater. It must also be shallow, clean, and clear.

The corals that make up a reef don't grow well below 130 feet. Deeper than that, it's too cold, dark, and still for them. They need sunshine, and they need the flow of the waves to bring their food to them. Each little tube-shaped coral animal has a mouth surrounded by fingerlike sensors. These tentacles catch tiny swimming animals in the gently flowing water.

Coral reefs are found in oceans around the world.

Huge coral reefs like underwater cliffs are made by tiny animals less than $\frac{1}{2}$ inch across. How do they do it?

Each little coral animal attaches itself to the skeletons of those that lived before it. As it grows, it takes calcium from the water and uses it to form a limestone skeleton. When it dies, its hard skeleton remains. Then a new coral animal attaches on top of it. Over time, these very tiny limestone skeletons form a large coral wall. A coral reef grows very slowly—its ridges may be only 3 feet higher in 1,000 years.

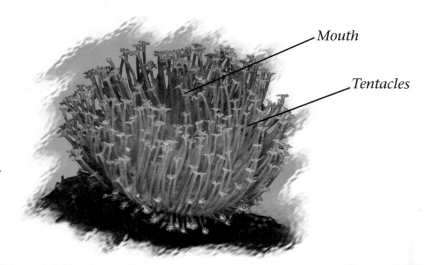

Mouth

Tentacles

CORAL

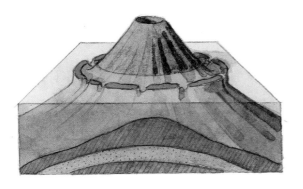

There are three kinds of reefs. A reef may grow around the edge of a volcanic island like fringe around a tablecloth. This is called a **fringing reef**. Most volcanic islands are ancient. Lava no longer flows from their craters.

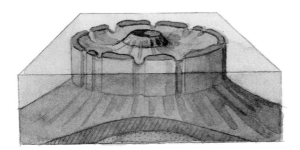

Over the years, the ocean floor may move, and the volcano may begin to sink. Water flows between the volcano and the reef, making a calm lagoon. Now the reef is called a **barrier reef**.

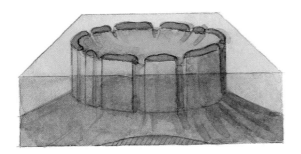

Finally the ancient volcano—crater, lava, and all—disappears. When the island slips under the water, only the reef can be seen. The ring it forms is a **coral atoll**.

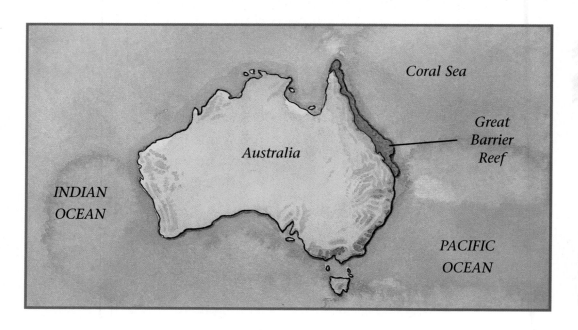

Find the Great Barrier Reef on a map or a globe. Like the Great Wall of China, it is large enough to be seen from space. No other reef is as rich with sea life as this one, the largest on Earth. Rare and colorful sea animals meander in and out of its coral gardens. Scuba divers love to visit this incredible reef to observe and photograph its strange and beautiful sea life. Here are some animals that make their homes in these warm waters.

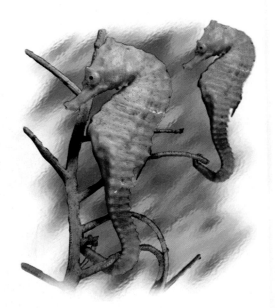

Sea Horse
Sea horses, like monkeys, have tails that can cling to plants. The males have a pouch in which they carry the eggs until they hatch. The babies use their "monkey tails" to cling together!

Green Sea Turtle

These huge turtles grow to be 300 pounds and may have 4-foot-long shells. Only the female ever comes ashore. Each year she digs a hole in the sand and lays about 100 eggs.

Longnose Butterfly Fish

These brightly colored fish have long snouts that they use to pluck food from the coral. At night they darken their bodies and sleep in coral caves.

Giant Clam

The giant clam has the biggest shell on Earth. At almost $\frac{1}{4}$ ton, it is also the largest animal without a backbone.

Crown-of-Thorns Sea Star

This big starfish feeds on coral. There are many more of them lately, so more damage is being done to the reefs.

Coral reefs are the gardens of the ocean. Clean, warm, gently moving water and sunlight keep them growing. Without these things, coral life will die, and the reefs will become barren piles of rock. Today, many coral reefs are threatened by pollution. They no longer have the clean water they need to grow in. To save the reefs, we will have to fight pollution. We must care for and preserve our beautiful gardens of the sea.

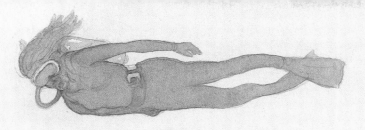

Think About It

1. Where do coral reefs grow?

2. How is a coral reef like a garden? How is it different from a garden?

3. Suppose you've been asked to write a report about one of the animals that live in the warm waters near a reef. Which animal would you choose? Write a paragraph about why you would choose that animal.

An Encounter with Space People

by Jeanette Mara

illustrated by Bonnie Matthews

One day a spaceship landed in our schoolyard and released two giant space people. When they invaded our gym class, things got really weird!

Miss Clancy boldly approached the space people. "What are you doing here?" she asked them.

The space people didn't say a thing. They just advanced on her with piercing looks.

This had to be a difficult experience for Miss Clancy. However, she stood in the center of the gym and faced them. "Vince," she said calmly, "I need your help."

118

I'm Vince, and Miss Clancy knew I could help because I study people from space. Standing by her side, I looked closely at the space people, who were twice our size. From their features, I could tell they were from Mars.

"Did you need to stop here?" I asked them. They nodded, looking very sincere.

"Maybe they stopped because they need help," I explained to Miss Clancy. Then I asked the Mars people, "Do you have a problem?" They both nodded, again seeming very sincere. I could tell this was a difficult experience for them, too. They needed our help, but they didn't want any publicity. They just wanted to get on with their trip.

"Can't they speak?" Miss Clancy asked me.

"No, so we can't interview them," I said.

One of the space giants put a finger on the pen in Miss Clancy's hand. Miss Clancy released the pen and a big pad of chart paper. The Mars person printed *V•R•MT*.

"Can you crack the code and make a translation?" Miss Clancy asked me. I didn't know, but I said I'd try. In a short time, I had it!

"They need food," I explained. "They've used up all their supplies." The space people nodded.

I would have liked to ask them about their space trip, but they seemed impatient. They didn't want us to interview them. They just wanted to eat.

Miss Clancy sent all of us to get food. We didn't know what the people on Mars ate, but we gathered what we had.

The Mars people didn't look happy about cheese slices, celery sticks, and apples. "Eat up," I said. "I promise you will survive."

The Mars people made weird faces as they ate. We could tell they didn't like our food, but we didn't say anything. We just let them fill up. When they finished, one of them printed *V•8•4•NRG*.

"Good," I said. "Will you be on your way now?"

The space people nodded, now looking happy. We followed them out to the spaceship and gave them more food for their trip.

The two gentle giants waved good-bye to everyone and got into their seats. They liked us, but they wanted to get on with their trip.

In no time, the spaceship lifted up, up, and away. We were sorry to see them go. Our encounter with people from Mars had been an experience we would not forget.

"Vince," Miss Clancy said, "how did you work out their code?"

"People from Mars like fun," I said. "That made me look for a code that would be fun. It works like something we write." I took the chart paper and printed *OK*.

Miss Clancy smiled. "I get it! They use the names of letters and numbers as words."

"Right, but there's one more thing to know. They use the letter *V* to mean *we*."

Miss Clancy wrote on the chart paper and held it up. "*EZ*," we read. Everyone laughed and agreed. "It's easy when you know the code!"

Translation: V•R•MT = We are empty;
V•8•4•NRG = We ate for energy.

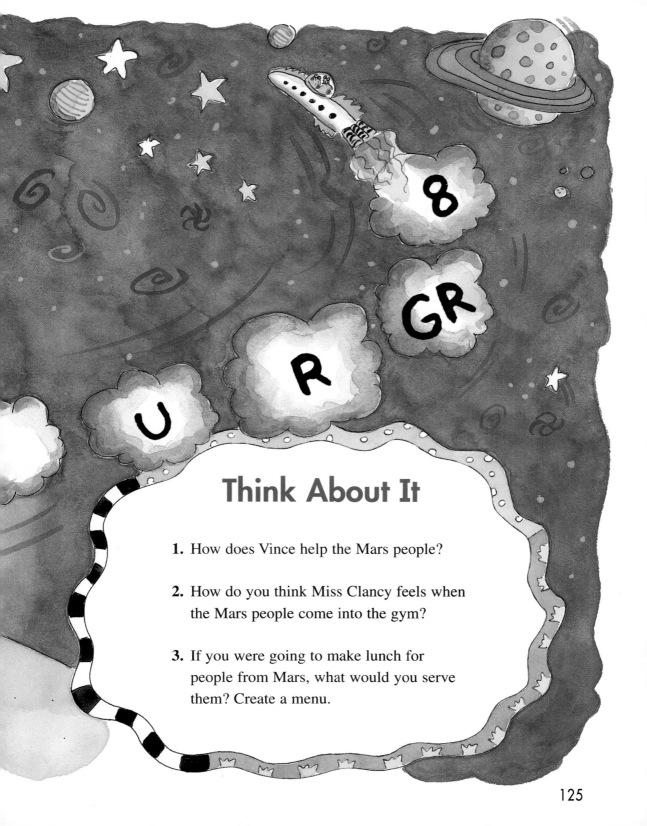

Think About It

1. How does Vince help the Mars people?

2. How do you think Miss Clancy feels when the Mars people come into the gym?

3. If you were going to make lunch for people from Mars, what would you serve them? Create a menu.

Peppermint-Peanut-Butter Fudge

by Pam Zollman

illustrated by Krieg Barrie

From our perch on the porch steps, Pearl and I could see all over the old homestead. Granny's birthday party looked like a county fair! All the relatives had gathered here for the occasion.

There would be sack races, three-legged races, and a baking contest—followed by the popular pie-eating contest! We planned to pack a lot of fun into the weekend. My sister and I should have been enjoying this happy occasion, but we weren't. We had no gift for Granny.

"Roy, I know!" said Pearl. "Let's make a tasty pan of fudge for her."

"Good choice, but you're looking at a boy who can't even boil water," I said.

Pearl said, "I'll show you how." In the kitchen, she put generous amounts of cocoa and other things into a pot. "You've been appointed to stir," she said. "Add some butter." I stirred in an entire jar of peanut butter.

Pearl was annoyed. I shrugged. "It's the same as butter, right?" I said.

127

"No!" replied Pearl loudly. "Oh, well—too late now." After the fudge mix boiled, she poured it into a pan.

As I stepped forward to see the result, Granny's cat ran in front of my feet. I jumped back, and my arm bumped the candy bowl. Yikes! Peppermints were adding themselves to the fudge mix!

For a brief moment I wanted to cry. "Surely I've spoiled it! Granny won't want peppermint-peanut-butter fudge."

"Don't despair," Pearl said in a kind voice. "It may be okay."

As soon as the fudge set, we sampled it. It was nice and moist, but I made a face. "It's too sweet. We'll have to throw it away."

"Let's go join in the contests," said Pearl. "We can feed the fudge to the pigs later."

Andy beat us in the sack race, and Sara won the pie-eating trophy. As we watched the relatives play table tennis, I brooded about one undeniable fact—we still had no gift for Granny.

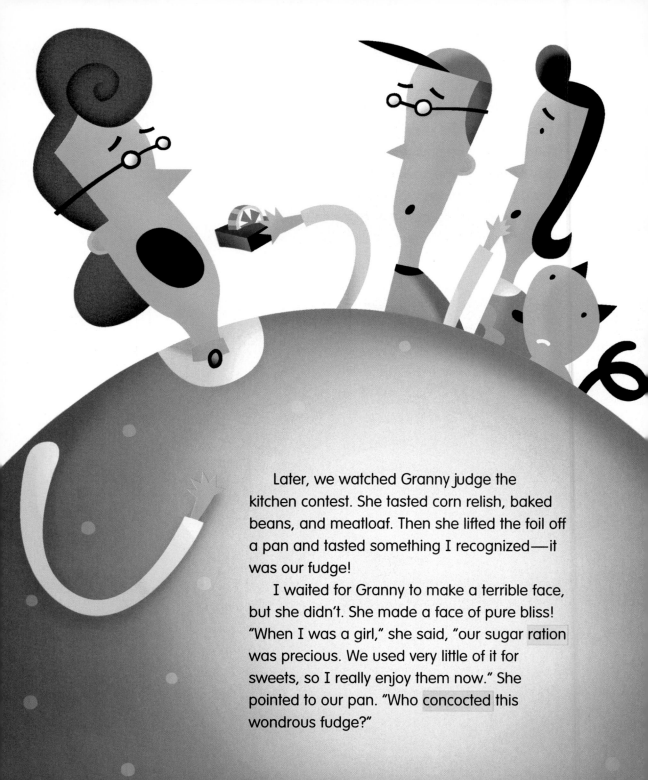

Later, we watched Granny judge the kitchen contest. She tasted corn relish, baked beans, and meatloaf. Then she lifted the foil off a pan and tasted something I recognized—it was our fudge!

I waited for Granny to make a terrible face, but she didn't. She made a face of pure bliss! "When I was a girl," she said, "our sugar ration was precious. We used very little of it for sweets, so I really enjoy them now." She pointed to our pan. "Who concocted this wondrous fudge?"

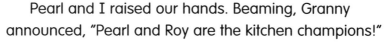

Pearl and I raised our hands. Beaming, Granny announced, "Pearl and Roy are the kitchen champions!"

"Happy Birthday, Granny," I said. "The fudge is your gift from us." I poured her a generous glass of milk. I had a feeling she'd need it!

Granny hugged us. "You two are my best gift, more precious than the most wondrous sweets!"

I winked at Pearl. "And we were worried about the fudge."

Pearl just grinned.

Think About It

1. Why don't Roy and Pearl like the fudge they made? Why does Granny like the fudge?

2. How do you think Roy and Pearl feel when they see Granny tasting their fudge? Why?

3. After her birthday party, Granny sends Roy and Pearl a thank-you letter. Write the thank-you letter she sends.

Just Jesting

A diner, while dining at Crewe,
Found quite a large mouse in his stew.
    Said the waiter, "Don't shout
    And wave it about,
Or the rest will be wanting one, too."

        A diner said, greatly annoyed,
        "My dinner I have not enjoyed.
            The cabbage was boiled,
            The pork chop was spoiled,
        And the flies I could not avoid."

There is an old cook in New York
Who insists you should always stew pork.
    He says he once tried
    To eat some that was fried
And claims he would rather chew cork.

133

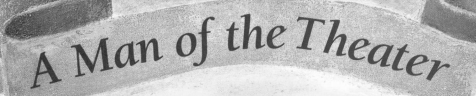

A Man of the Theater

by
Meish Goldish
illustrated by Melanie Hall

In the 1600s, there were no TV shows or films to entertain people. However, there were plenty of plays to see in theaters. In France, many plays were created by a popular writer named Molière.

Audiences of Molière's time lavished praise on him. He remains highly respected today. In fact, many have called Molière "The Shakespeare of France."

Molière was born in 1622 into a well-to-do family. In time, he was sent to a college to be taught law. However, Molière did not wish to become a lawyer. He was much more drawn to drama.

When he was 21, Molière began to put on plays with three fellow actors. The group went from town to town to perform. Their stage was a wagon bed drawn by a horse. One member was a patron of the group. He helped pay the cost of the shows. All four were shareholders in their small acting company.

Later Molière and his actors performed in Paris. They dismantled their rolling stage. Now they followed their cherished dreams of fame and riches. At that time in France, however, many people looked down on actors. They were critical of all dramas.

After about a year in Paris, the actors ran out of money. Molière, unable to pay back what he had borrowed, was jailed. He was not in jail long, however. His family paid what he owed, and Molière left Paris.

Together again, the four actors launched new plays all over France. Molière created, directed, and acted in the shows they put on.

At last, in 1658, Molière's luck changed. The new king of France saw one of his plays. He asked Molière to create new dramas as royal entertainment. He even gave Molière a permanent theater in which to put on his plays.

From then on, Molière was respected. His first play for the king was a comedy. It poked fun at the haughty way some rich people behaved. The audience applauded loudly. Molière's work had caught on.

Over the next twelve years, Molière created many more comedies. They were based on the flaws and faults of people in real life. Molière made these very funny on stage. The applause for his plays grew louder and longer.

The king cherished Molière as an adornment to his court. No longer did Molière have to worry about getting his plays produced.

Not everyone liked his work, however. The people that Molière poked fun at were not happy with his plays. One group complained because one of its members was shown as a fraud. Even the king banned that play until Molière agreed to change parts of it.

139

Besides writing his plays, Molière acted in them as long as he lived. In 1673, he became ill while performing and died later that night.

In 1680, the main theater in France was named "The House of Molière." Since then, theaters everywhere have been congested with huge crowds when Molière's plays are performed. To this day, his name is known to theater-goers around the world.

Think About It

1. What topics did Molière write about in his plays?

2. Why did audiences change their minds about Molière's plays?

3. If there had been television in the 1600s, a reporter might have interviewed Molière about his career. Write some questions and answers for an interview.

MY IMAGINARY WORLD

WRITTEN AND ILLUSTRATED BY ISTVAN BANYAI

How did I become an illustrator?
It started like this. When I was a boy
growing up in Hungary, people didn't
have TVs in their homes. We did lots
of other things for fun. I rode my
bicycle almost every day. Sometimes
I would cross one of the seven bridges
spanning the Danube River and ride
into downtown Budapest.

I had no brothers or sisters, so
I often played alone. Perhaps that
is why I dreamed up such a vivid
imaginary world.

My mother died when I was born, so my grandmother raised me. She had so many wonderful old things in her house. There were wooden boxes full of old photos, ancient maps, and other mementos of times past.

Of all my grandmother's old things, her slide lantern was my favorite. She would let me put the beautiful hand-painted glass slides into it myself. Then the light inside it would flash their images onto my wall.

When I was a child, I spent much time drawing. I had a good teacher who encouraged me.

Like an author, I made up stories—some scary and some not—as I sketched. Sometimes I invented entire armies to battle each other in my sketches. These drawings were scary, but others were funny and made people laugh. Using my pencil, I could enter my imaginary world anytime I wanted.

Istvan Banyai

Later, I went to art classes. I learned about many different styles and experimented with using charcoal and pastels. However, I found that using a pencil was still my favorite way to draw. Now I've developed a style of my own, but I always begin my work in pencil.

First, I make a series of drawings. Then I transfer them to clear plastic sheets. Finally, I paint bright colors inside the lines on the back of the plastic. The pictures I did for the book *Zoom* took me more than 120 hours to complete!

Illustrating is my job. I wake up every morning
and take a shower in ideas. I burn my toast, and the
crumbs on the counter remind me of the dots my
pencil makes. Sometimes I start the sketches for
a new book by making dots and then staring at
them. Before long, they begin to look like
something—perhaps tiny planets
floating in space.

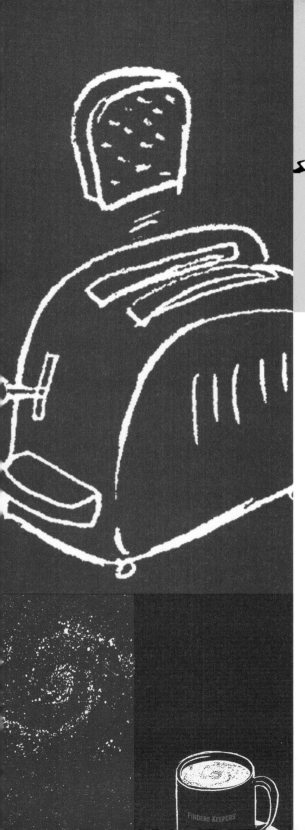

Suddenly I leave behind the mess in the kitchen. I move from the real world to a wondrous imaginary place. Here no one ever burns the toast, and the sun shines down on a morning that never ends.

I am the author of my own stories. I make up the characters and give them things to do. I draw the house where they live. The books I illustrate are windows into my imaginary world—a place you are always welcome to visit.

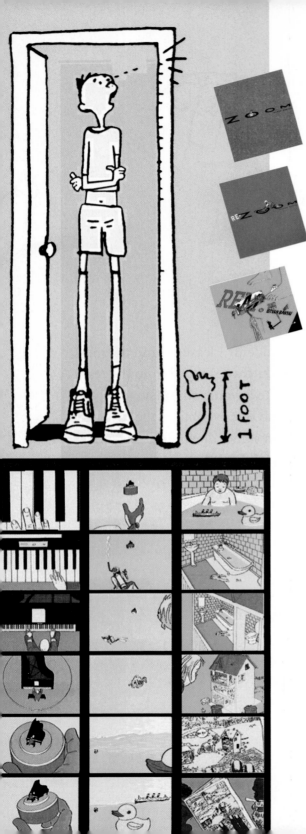

Books by Istvan Banyai:

Zoom
Re-Zoom
REM (Rapid Eye Movement)
by Istvan Banyai
(Viking/Penguin)

Poems for Children Nowhere Near Old Enough to Vote
by Carl Sandburg
illustrated by Istvan Banyai
(Knopf)

Think About It

1. Which parts of Istvan Banyai's childhood helped him become an illustrator?

2. How does Istvan Banyai feel about his work as an illustrator? How can you tell?

3. If you had a chance to meet Istvan Banyai, what else would you want to know about him and his work? Write at least four questions you would ask him.

Read It in Reverse!

Here are some examples of palindromes. *Palindrome* comes from Greek words that mean "again" (*palin*) and "running" (*dromos*), so you might say that palindromes "run back again." In other words, you'll find that they read just the same from right to left as they do from left to right. Try it!

Nurse, so no noses run?

Was it a rat I saw?

Can I attain a "C"?

A tip: save Eva's pita.

Ma has a ham.

Norah's moods, alas, doom Sharon.

Mash Sid a radish, Sam.

A nut for a jar of tuna?

"Delia was ill!" Lisa wailed.

Draw Della too tall, Edward.

WITH LOVE FROM *Ella*

by Susan M. Fischer
illustrated by Stan Shaw

**An Imaginary Letter
from Ella Fitzgerald to a Fan**

January 28, 1992

Dear Drew,

Thank you for your nice letter. I had to pause to smile when you called me your hero. You flatter me! I think it's grand that you want to be a composer. So, you want to know about my career? I'll be glad to tell you a little about my life.

I was born in 1918, yet I am much like you, Drew. We both adore music and have been surrounded by it from an early age.

My childhood was a happy one. My mother and I lived in New York near a pawnshop and a produce market. From the time I was a little girl, I loved to sing at church. I also sang with my friends on our front stoop in the afternoons after school. Soon I could imitate the styles of singers who were familiar from the radio. Some of their voices were smooth, and some were gravelly. I had good pitch—I could sing each note in perfect tune. However, what I really loved to do was dance.

151

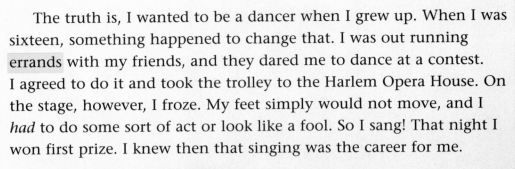

The truth is, I wanted to be a dancer when I grew up. When I was sixteen, something happened to change that. I was out running errands with my friends, and they dared me to dance at a contest. I agreed to do it and took the trolley to the Harlem Opera House. On the stage, however, I froze. My feet simply would not move, and I *had* to do some sort of act or look like a fool. So I sang! That night I won first prize. I knew then that singing was the career for me.

My confidence grew, and I competed in more contests and won them all. One night a familiar-looking man came to hear me sing. He was Chick Webb, the leader of a jazz band and a well-known figure in the music industry. He liked what he heard and hired me to sing with his band! He helped me develop a style and rhythm all my own. I rehearsed every day. Chick introduced me to numerous people important in the industry, and this gave my career a boost. I was becoming an international star.

153

Chick was also a composer, and together we wrote numerous songs. In 1938, I recorded one of them. It was called "A-Tisket, A-Tasket." It sold a million copies in only a couple of weeks, and it is still one of my best-known songs. When Chick died, I felt so blue. I became the leader of the band, and we played our music everywhere. The public loved us, as jazz was very popular. After three years, however, I paused to consider my career. It was time for me to leave the band and go solo.

I sang all over the world. I could sing any style of music, and I invented a style of my own. I used my voice to make sounds like those of a musical instrument. This new style I called "scat" singing, and music experts loved it. The public loved it, too. It became part of jazz history. So not only is jazz a part of me—I am a part of jazz!

Be true to your dreams, Drew, and maybe one day you can compose a song for me. Thank you again for your letter.

With love from Ella

In her long career, Ella Fitzgerald recorded more than 200 songs and earned 13 Grammys. Some say she was the greatest singer of all time. She appeared on stage for the last time in 1993. Ella Fitzgerald died on June 15, 1996. Over the years Ella gathered numerous awards and honors. In 1995 she became a member of the National Women's Hall of Fame. The "First Lady of Song" will always be remembered for her "scat" style of jazz singing.

Think About It

1. How did Ella Fitzgerald develop her love of music?

2. Why did she become a singer instead of a dancer?

3. When Drew is asked to write a paragraph about a famous American, he chooses Ella Fitzgerald. In his paragraph, he must explain his choice. Write the paragraph Drew turns in to his teacher.

LOURDES LÓPEZ:
Ballet Star

by Doris Licameli

illustrated by Rosemary Fox

Lourdes López (LAWRD•es LOH•pez) was born in Cuba on May 2, 1958. A year later, the López family migrated to Florida, where Lourdes grew up.

When Lourdes was 5, her doctor ordered special shoes to correct a problem with her feet. At the shoe store, Lourdes spied ballet shoes. While the clerk wrapped her plain, brown shoes, Lourdes wriggled her toes into the ballet shoes. *Oh, to be a ballerina!*

Soon Lourdes had a happy surprise. The doctor also ordered dance lessons to make her legs stronger. Lourdes began taking ballet classes. The teacher could see that Lourdes had real talent.

When she was 8, Lourdes began to study with Alexander Nigodoff. He introduced his students to story ballets such as *Cinderella* and *Sleeping Beauty*. He showed them the steps of dances from those ballets. Lourdes enjoyed dance more than ever!

Dancing six days a week left little time for fun. "Why do you devote so much time to ballet?" her friends asked. It made Lourdes a little sad, knowing that they didn't understand her love of dance.

Then Lourdes performed at a school event. As her friends watched, Lourdes demonstrated her artistic skill. When her dance ended, her friends cheered. Lourdes bowed in triumph.

Later, Lourdes won a full scholarship to the School of American Ballet. She was only 14 when she said good-bye to her family. She moved to New York City with her sister, Terry.

Lourdes took classes in ballet technique every day. She worked hard and learned fast. Very soon, George Balanchine, the school's founder, took note of Lourdes. Under his coaching, her talent bloomed.

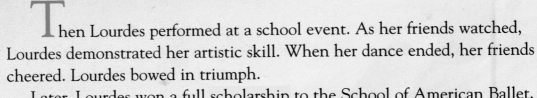

NEW YORK SCHOOL

RECOGNIZES

Lourdes Ló

161

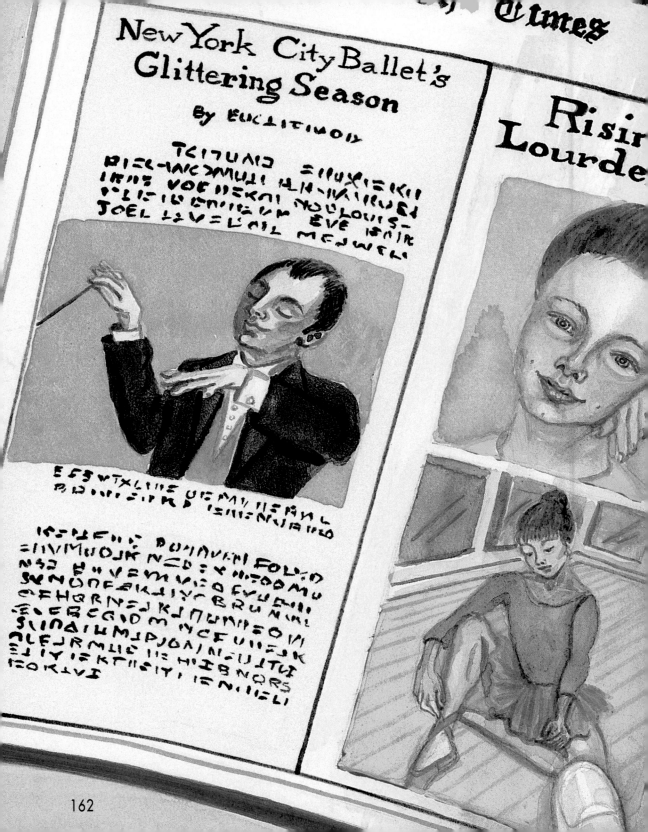

New York City Ballet's Glittering Season

By EUCLITIMON

Risir
Lourde

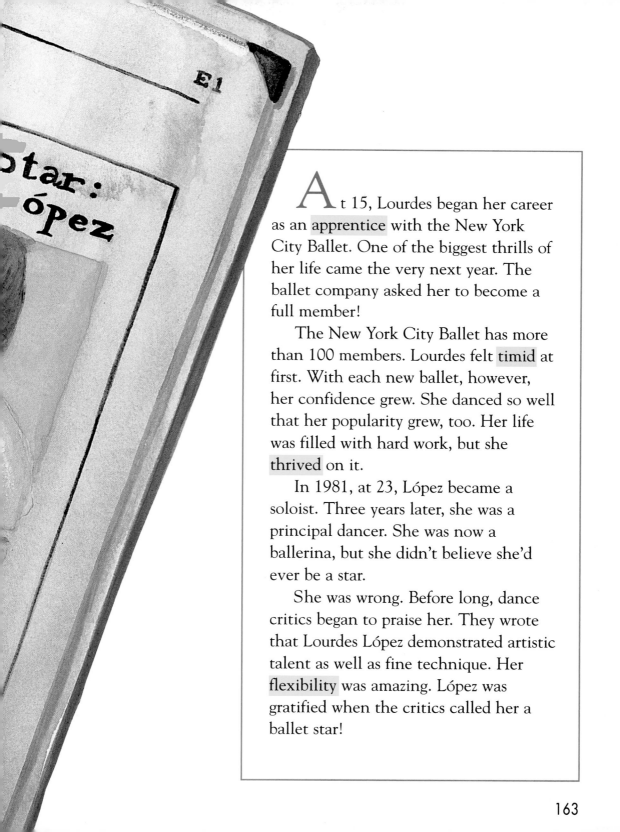

At 15, Lourdes began her career as an apprentice with the New York City Ballet. One of the biggest thrills of her life came the very next year. The ballet company asked her to become a full member!

The New York City Ballet has more than 100 members. Lourdes felt timid at first. With each new ballet, however, her confidence grew. She danced so well that her popularity grew, too. Her life was filled with hard work, but she thrived on it.

In 1981, at 23, López became a soloist. Three years later, she was a principal dancer. She was now a ballerina, but she didn't believe she'd ever be a star.

She was wrong. Before long, dance critics began to praise her. They wrote that Lourdes López demonstrated artistic talent as well as fine technique. Her flexibility was amazing. López was gratified when the critics called her a ballet star!

In 1988, Lourdes hurt her foot. She knew that this might threaten her dance career. Luckily, however, she made a fast recovery. She returned to the stage in triumph, her popularity higher than ever.

Lourdes stopped dancing with the New York City Ballet in 1997. Now she devotes her time to working with the children of New York City. Lourdes shows them what ballet can mean to their lives.

Think About It

1. How did Lourdes López's dancing career develop in New York City?

2. Do you think Lourdes López would have become a ballet star even if the doctor had not ordered dance lessons for her? Tell why you think as you do.

3. What do you think Lourdes López might have written in her diary on the day a dance critic first called her a star? Write her diary entry.

Certain Steps

by Charlene Norman
illustrated by Shelly Meridith

"Vote for Al. He's a pal!" Al said, making *V*'s for victory with his fingers. "You and I should team up on this campaign, Murphy. Then I know I'd beat Casey in the student council election."

"What's your platform?" Murphy asked.

"Maybe I'll stand on a chair when I give my speech."

Murphy shook his head. "A platform is what you plan to do if you're elected."

"My campaign comes first," Al said. "I plan to take certain steps so all the kids will know who I am."

The next day Al showed up carrying posters with his photo and pencils with *Vote for Al* on them. His portrait was on his T-shirt, too, along with the same message.

"What's your platform? What do you plan to do for your fellow students?" Murphy asked as they hung posters.

Al laughed. "Cut out all homework! Here, take a bunch of these pencils. I'm going to get the crossing guard to endorse my campaign." As he left, Al made an A-Okay sign with his hand and called back, "Certain steps, easy win!"

NicE HAt

Abraham Who?

Murphy had seldom seen his buddy act so obnoxious. He grew concerned about Al's "certain steps" and hung his posters in an uncertain mood.

A portrait of Abraham Lincoln standing in front of one of his residences caught Murphy's eye. He felt the President's gaze upon him. Was it challenging him to stand up for what was right? "I'll help Al run a good campaign," he vowed silently.

Then he noticed some graffiti on the wall, luckily just in pencil. He used one of Al's pencils to erase it. Some kids stopped to help and happily kept the pencils.

Murphy picked up trash around the playground while he waited for Al to finish his morning patrol job. Other kids noticed and joined Murphy.

On the way to class, Murphy gave Al some ideas for ways to improve things for students.

"I don't think so, Murphy," Al said. "Those ideas sound like too much work."

Murphy spoke sadly but firmly. "Al, I know those are the kind of steps a candidate should be taking." He looked down and apologized. "I'm sorry, but I just can't work on a campaign that promises no homework."

After lunch, Murphy was sitting on a bench outside, reading with a first grader. Al nodded to Murphy and then turned to whisper to several girls. They all turned to look as Al pointed to Murphy.

During geography, Murphy heard whispered phrases that included his name. Kids he considered friends stared at him and giggled. Murphy had felt certain he'd taken the right step to refuse to help Al. Now, however, the stares and whispers increased his mood of uncertainty. Should he apologize and support Al's campaign?

Later in the day the candidates gave their speeches. Casey promised Pizza Fridays. Then Al spoke.

"A student who cares a lot," he said, stretching his arms wide for emphasis, "will organize student volunteers. You can join the group of your choice to pick up trash, remove graffiti, or read with first graders once a week. Vote for the person I'm voting for. Cross off Al and write in Murphy. You'll seldom have a leader who cares as much."

Kids laughed and clapped as Murphy grinned. Al smiled and shook his hand. Then the teacher said it was time to vote.

Think About It

1. Why does Murphy finally refuse to help Al with his campaign?

2. How do you think Murphy feels when he hears other kids giggling and whispering phrases that include his name?

3. Think about the main character, Murphy. Make a web with words that tell what Murphy thinks, likes, and does. Then using your web as a plan, write a paragraph about Murphy.

The Politician's Bookshelf

Running a Tough Campaign by Wynn M. Awl

Phrases to Keep Your Audience Laughing by Ima Chucklin

Using Phone Volunteers by Bugs M. Constantly

Posing for Your Campaign Photos by The Brothers Grinn

What to Do When the Campaign Gets Dull by Borden Blue

Want to Improve Your TV Image? by Sawyer Ads

Effective Campaign Platforms by Promise M. Damoon

Getting Large Crowds for Your Appearances
by Phillip D. Seats

Quest for a Healthy World

by Carol Storment
illustrated by Josephine Hill

Jonas Salk always wanted to know everything about the world around him—his first excited words were "Dirt, dirt!" When he grew up, he planned to be a lawyer. Before long, however, Salk realized that he cared more about the laws of nature. It was a lucky day for people around the world when he switched from law school to medical school.

Jonas Salk did not intend to become a doctor who treated people, but he took all the training to do so. He really wanted to be a medical scientist.

While still a student, Salk helped work on a vaccine to prevent influenza, or flu. He was very interested in this project because he wanted to test something that one of his medical teachers had claimed. This teacher had stated that illnesses caused by bacteria could be prevented by injecting people with killed germs for those diseases. He insisted, however, that this method didn't work for illnesses, such as the flu, that are caused by viruses.

Dr. Salk at work in his lab

1914
Jonas Edward Salk
born in New York City

Salk suspected that a killed-virus vaccine had been tried without success. That didn't mean the method could never succeed, he reasoned. This seemed like the right time to go ahead and try it again.

Through careful experiments, Salk found that it *was* possible to use killed viruses. In time he developed a flu vaccine that has saved thousands of lives.

When Salk was a boy in New York City, the spread of flu threatened people's lives each year. Now a flu threat can be stopped in its tracks, thanks to his "flu shot."

THE NEWSPAPER

Salk

Plan a

MAGAZINE

Dr. Jonas Salk

VACCINE

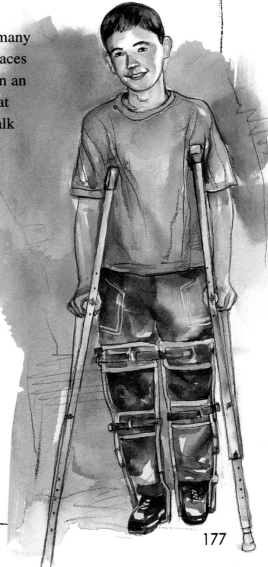

Polio was much, much worse. After it hit, many
people could not walk without unwieldy leg braces
and crutches. Some lived a life of immobility in an
iron lung. This was a tank with an air pump that
helped them breathe. Many people died. Dr. Salk
knew that his next quest would be to develop a
vaccine for this illness.

The research required many experiments
and much time to decipher the enormous
amount of data. Dr. Salk hit many dead
ends, but he always looked at them as
chances to learn.

After Dr. Salk's dramatic discovery, he
became well known. He was astonished and
dismayed by his fame. It was hard for him to
keep on with his work, and that was what he
wanted to do most.

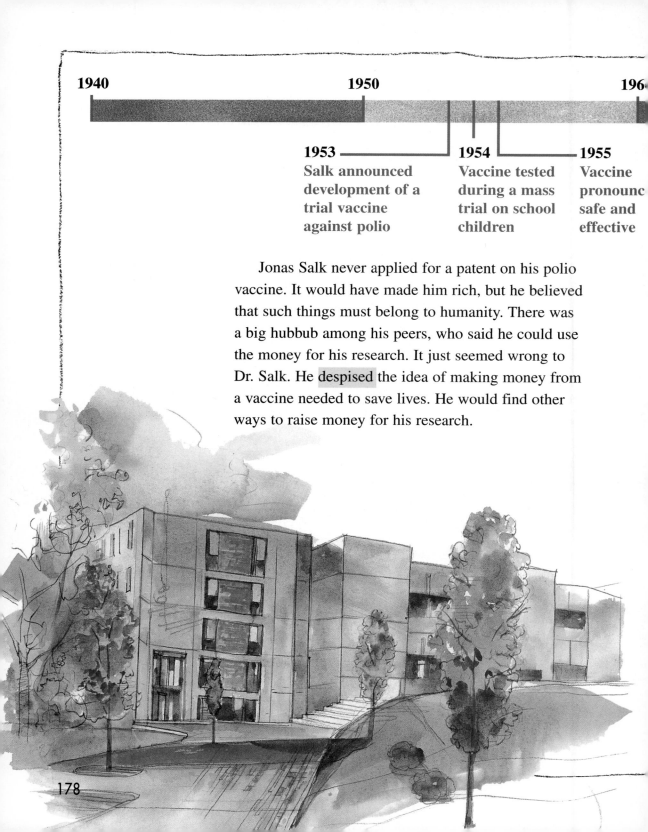

1940	1950	196

1953 ——— Salk announced development of a trial vaccine against polio

1954 — Vaccine tested during a mass trial on school children

1955 — Vaccine pronounc safe and effective

Jonas Salk never applied for a patent on his polio vaccine. It would have made him rich, but he believed that such things must belong to humanity. There was a big hubbub among his peers, who said he could use the money for his research. It just seemed wrong to Dr. Salk. He despised the idea of making money from a vaccine needed to save lives. He would find other ways to raise money for his research.

1977
Dr. Salk awarded
the Presidential
Medal of Freedom

Looking back on his life, Dr. Salk remembered teachers who were important to him. Some of them were from his early school years. He also had a favorite instructor in medical school.

In many ways, however, he felt that his best teacher was his mother. She came to America as a young girl and had to work to help her family. She did not have the chance to go to school, but she saw to it that her children did. She knew what a dramatic difference it would make to their lives. It was Jonas Salk's mother who started him on the path that led to his lifesaving achievements.

1995
Dr. Salk dies
at age 81

Dr. Salk was asked what he would tell children and teenagers who were thinking about career choices. He said that each one of us has something to give to life on earth. That gift is different for everyone. The best way to have a sense of purpose is to first know ourselves. We need to know what we care about and then work for that dream.

Jonas Salk believed that it is important for us to do something that helps humanity as well as ourselves. His own quest to develop vaccines against viruses has helped the health of the entire world.

Think About It

1. What did Jonas Salk achieve in his quest for a healthy world?

2. Why do you think Jonas Salk chose to become a medical scientist rather than a doctor?

3. Think about Dr. Salk's accomplishments. Choose one or two you feel are important and write Dr. Salk a thank-you letter.

Dr. Salk

Pete's Great Invention

by Linda Lott   illustrated by Beppie Giacobbe

It was ten after eight when Pete slipped into his seat.

"Pete," Miss Deighton said with a scowl, "you are tardy again."

"He wants to break his record," Mark called out. "He's been late eight days in a row now."

The class giggled, but Pete's face turned red.

"That's enough racket," Miss Deighton said. "Pete, please make an effort to be on time from now on."

It wasn't that Pete didn't care about being late. He simply couldn't seem to get up in the morning.

The loud noise of the nearby refinery starting up for the day didn't wake him. He slept soundly through the screech of the early morning freight train, too. A little alarm clock was no match for that kind of deep sleep because Pete could turn it off without ever really waking up.

When Pete was asleep, a mysterious veil seemed to muffle all his senses. If he took a nap after he came home, even the smell of a great steak dinner wouldn't wake him.

Pete was afraid his grades would slip if he continued to be tardy every day. What could he do?

Then Pete had an idea. Everyone had to make an original invention for the class invention fair. Why not solve two problems at once by inventing a super alarm? If his invention was a success, he would never be late again, and he would also get a good grade from Miss Deighton.

Pete wrote out a detailed description of what he planned to do. He drew and labeled a diagram. Then he set to work.

First, Pete insulated one wall of his bedroom with blankets. His alarm should not wake his grandma in the next room.

Next, he took down a hanging model plane and threaded a rope through its hook. He attached pots and pans to one end of the rope and shook them. What a racket they made!

Then Pete tied a weight to the other end of the rope and raised the pots and pans. He set the weight on top of his alarm clock's switch.

Pete's plan was that when he sleepily fumbled to turn off his alarm, he would knock over the weight. This would jerk the rope and jangle the pots and pans.

Pete's family couldn't wait to see his mysterious invention. His dad reminded him of one thing.

"Don't forget about the cat! He prowls around the house every night, and you wouldn't want him to trigger your alarm too soon."

Pete tried making a cardboard partition to fit around his bed, but the cat easily jumped over it. Oh well—he could just shut his door at night.

When Pete let his family see his invention, his mom grumbled a little about her pots and pans. Then she thought about their hectic mornings and said, "Never mind. If it works, it'll be worth it!"

A week later, Pete submitted his super alarm to the class invention fair. He set it up, read aloud the description, and demonstrated how it worked. His classmates covered their ears, but they knew a useful invention when they heard one.

"Now, that's what I call an original idea!" Mark called out.

The class cheered loudly to show that they agreed with Mark. Miss Deighton agreed with Mark, too. She winked at Pete.

"I already knew your invention was a great success," she said. "You haven't been late once since you invented it!"

Think About It

1. What does Pete invent? How does Miss Deighton know that Pete's invention is a success?

2. Do you think other people would be interested in using Pete's great invention? Why or why not?

3. Pete wants to try selling his invention to other people. He writes an ad to put on some posters. Write the ad that Pete may have written.

Science Class Fun

Why did the toad bring a bar of soap to school?
    The weather forecast was predicting showers.

Why did the polar bear wear an extra coat across his chest?
    He heard that a cold front was coming.

What kind of smart jokes did the duckling make at recess?
    Wisequacks.

Why did the iguana ask the whole fifth-grade science class to stand on ladders?
    Somebody told him his science grade should be higher.

Why did the worker bee step on the scales during school vacation?
    He wanted to relax and get a-weigh.

Why did the herring go to school on Saturday?
    He wanted to be in a class by himself.

One of a Kind

by Ann W. Phillips   illustrated by Patrick Joseph O'Malley

What Jenna liked best about school was Friday afternoons. That was when Mr. Lee would say, "Time for the widget game!"

The widget was whatever object Mr. Lee was thinking of. Teams would ask questions to help them identify the widget. The winners got points added to their column on the board—points that counted toward a pizza party. The pizza was bait, Jenna knew, but it was good bait.

Some kids thought the game was dumb, but Jenna didn't think so. To Jenna, it was like a mystery, and she saw herself as a word detective on assignment.

Andy's team didn't think the game was dumb, either. They had vowed they'd beat Jenna's team.

Jenna's team was ahead, but not by much. They had to win—their reputation and their honor were at stake. They would let nothing sidetrack them. Jenna and Peter and Holly had taken a solemn oath: "Pizza or bust!"

"Here's your first clue," said Mr. Lee. "The widget doesn't whistle. Questions?"

The teams took turns asking questions. This time Andy's team went first. Jenna leaned forward and squinted in serious concentration. When a team felt ready to guess what the widget was, someone would blow his or her kazoo. You had to be pretty certain, though. If you guessed wrong, your team was out of the game.

"Is it smaller than the room?" Andy asked.

"Yes."

Jenna chewed her thumb and listened to the answers with complete concentration.

"Is it bigger than a book?"

"Yes."

"Can you comb your hair with it?" That was Colin's team—they were never serious. They got a *no*.

"Does it have hair?" A few laughs—and a *no*.

The questions flew. "Is it something you read?" Another *no*.

"Can you eat it for lunch?" *No* again.

At last it was Jenna's team's turn, and Peter asked an important question.

"Is it one of a kind, or are there lots of them?"

"One of a kind," said Mr. Lee with a big grin. "Definitely one of a kind."

Bingo! Like a flash of light, the answer came to Jenna, and she grabbed for her kazoo. It rolled off her desk into the aisle. Out of the corner of her eye, she could see Andy reaching for his kazoo. There was no time to check with the rest of her team. Jenna dove into the aisle, snatched up her kazoo, and blew it.

"Jenna," Mr. Lee said, "would you like to identify the widget, or are you just rolling in the aisle?"

Everyone laughed as Jenna scrambled to her feet. What if she was wrong and her guess was dumb? There would go the pizza party for everyone. Squinting at the floor, she became absorbed in staring at the toes of her shoes. Her brain was numb.

"We're listening, Jenna," prompted Mr. Lee.

Jenna took a deep breath, looked up at the teacher, and pointed. "You," she said at last. "You are the widget, Mr. Lee."

195

"Correct!" Mr. Lee said, beaming at her. "I can't whistle, and I'm smaller than the room but bigger than a book. You can't comb your hair with me, read me, or eat me for lunch. Furthermore, I don't have hair—well, not much!" He grinned as the kids giggled. "I am definitely one of a kind."

"Pizza! Pizza! Pizza!" Jenna's team cheered. "Hooray for Jenna!"

Jenna was beaming, too. Another widget assignment successfully completed by a winning word detective!

Think About It

1. How does Jenna figure out that Mr. Lee is the widget?

2. How does Jenna feel just before she gives her answer? How does she feel right after she gives her answer?

3. Write a sentence telling what classroom object you would choose if you were the leader in the widget game. Then write five questions you would ask to help identify a widget.

WHAT A

MONDAY

Because of the recent dispute among our leaders, I decided to keep this diary. I was thoroughly scornful of their proposed Detroit project. What is the sense in digging up a long-ago city named Detroit? I thought my robots could be put to better use on the moon-orbiter project.

Anyway, the Detroit dig started today. I'll record the results of the week-long project in this diary.

According to the experts, "cars" were made in this city centuries ago. I wonder what they were for.

198

TIME IT WAS!

by Jared Jansen • illustrated by Chris Lensch

TUESDAY

It seems the so-called cars were also called automobiles. The robots located a museum filled with them, and I'm sorry now that I was scornful of this project. I must admit I'm really getting into it.

I found out that for almost two centuries, people went from place to place sitting in these automobiles. When the jet tube came into being, people's bodies became adjusted to horizontal travel. How odd to think of traveling sitting upright! I tried sitting in one of the automobiles today, and it was mighty tough to get comfortable.

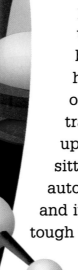

WEDNESDAY

I suspect that I am bigger than the average person who made regular use of the automobile.

The car I finally squeezed myself into was a 2002 deluxe convertible. It must have been terribly slow. Its top speed was only about 180 miles per hour, according to the dials behind the thing they called a steering wheel. My brother's 12-year-old daughter goes roughly 300 miles per hour in her junior jet tube.

The dials also indicated that the model I sat in had "air bags." I suppose they were some kind of equipment for breathing. I expect I'll find out when I look through the automobile manual.

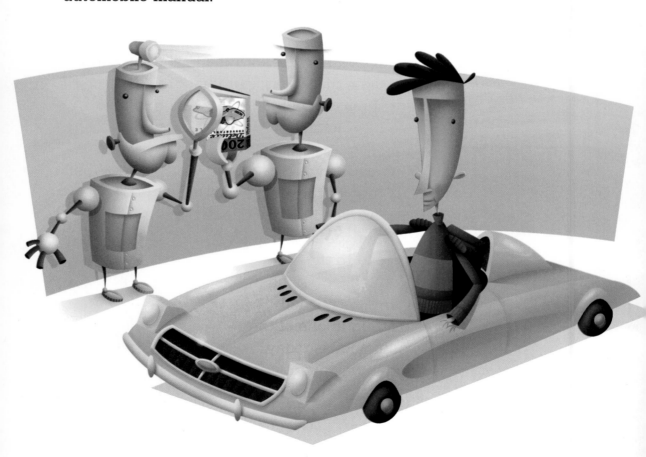

THURSDAY

The manual was amusing. It talked loftily about the wonders of the convertible. I calculated that it used the word *wonderful* in every third sentence. I also calculated that this "mechanical wonder" was really a mechanical nightmare.

The convertible's warranty was for only one hundred thousand miles or ten years, whichever came first. That means the average person today would go through almost twenty of them. Why, our personalized jet tubes last a lifetime, if not longer!

Tonight I'll read the part about the air bags. What I can't figure out is how people could see anything with bags over their heads.

Friday

Well, I found out what
the air bags were for. No,
people didn't put them over
their heads for breathing purposes. I
had that all wrong. The truth turned out to be
even stranger than I thought!

It seems that, back in those days, they had open tracks for
the automobiles to run on. Cars traveled side by side and both
ways on these tracks. Every now and then, accidents would
happen, and that's where the air bags came in. In a crash,
they exploded into pillows!

I'm glad our jet tubes go through one-way tunnels one at a
time. Air bags sound a little too exciting for me.

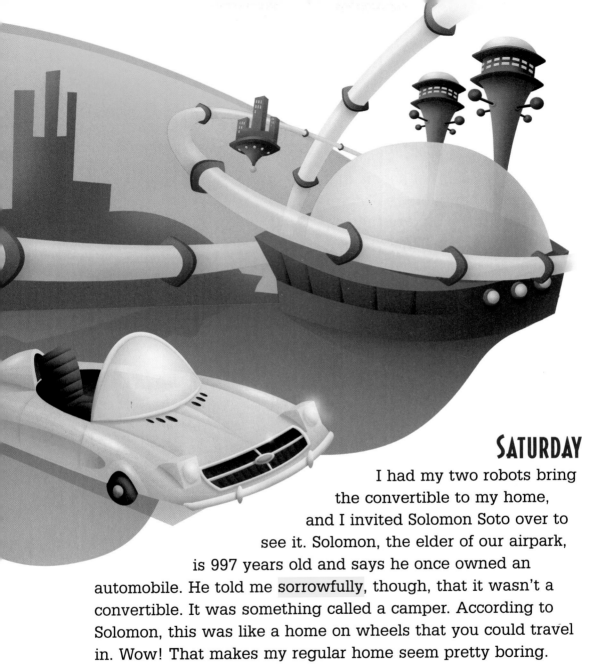

SATURDAY

I had my two robots bring the convertible to my home, and I invited Solomon Soto over to see it. Solomon, the elder of our airpark, is 997 years old and says he once owned an automobile. He told me sorrowfully, though, that it wasn't a convertible. It was something called a camper. According to Solomon, this was like a home on wheels that you could travel in. Wow! That makes my regular home seem pretty boring.

Solomon claims that he can get the convertible running. We won't be able to go anywhere, but we can listen to a CD we found in it. The CD is a shiny, round thing that Solomon says has music on it.

SUNDAY

The CD is fantastic! It's called "Millennium Bash!" It seems that people back then were really excited about the start of the second millennium. They'd be surprised to know that we're getting ready to celebrate the third millennium!

As we listened to the CD, Solomon nonchalantly broke into a shuffle that he called dancing. Before I even realized it, I'd joined him in moving to the beat—and it felt good!

"Those were the days!" Solomon said with a chuckle. Although I wasn't around then, I had to agree. Those people knew how to have fun. What a time it was!

Think About It

1. What information did the man and his robots uncover in their dig?

2. What did the diary writer like most about the "old days" around the year 2000? What did he like least?

3. Suppose the man in "What a Time It Was!" came with his robots to dig in *your* hometown. What would he find? What would he think of it? Write about your ideas.

A Safe Harbor

by Susan McCloskey

illustrated by David Christiana

My name is Manolo Sánchez (mah•NOH•loh SAHN•chez), and as a child I lived in a small Spanish port called Palos (PAH•los). I liked to stroll down to the harbor and listen to the sailors' reports about their voyages. I never grew weary of their tales, for I wanted to be a sailor, too! I got my chance when Papá took a job on the *Santa María* (SAHN•tah mah•REE•ah).

Undoubtedly you have heard of that ship. It, along with the *Pinta* (PEEN•tah) and the *Niña* (NEEN•yah), sailed under the command of our Captain General, Christopher Columbus. Although he didn't plan it that way, the trip led to the settlement of the New World!

Papá was hired as a
cook, and I begged to go with
him. "I can help you cook!" I told him.
"I can help the sailors! I will do anything!"
Mamá disliked the idea of my going. "You
tell me that Captain Columbus says the world
is round," she said. "If that's so, it will be easy
enough to sail downhill. But let me remind you
that your return trip will be uphill. What then?
How will your ship remain upright all the
way around the world?"

In spite of Mamá's fears, when
the *Santa María* lifted anchor, I
was aboard.

As we left the harbor, I waved to my unhappy mamá until she faded into the horizon. Then I turned my back on the land and gazed upon the calm waters of the vast blue sea.

My job was to help Papá cook. In my spare time I helped the crew. I scrubbed the deck, I tied and untied ropes, and I carried buckets of water. Though the sailors liked me, they often teased me for being small. This didn't discourage me in the least.

One day a terrible storm came up. Waves
nearly flooded the deck, and the ship tipped
left and right, struggling to stay upright.
Water seeping between the beams made us
fear that the ship would sink. Danger from
the storm lurked everywhere.

Suddenly, a strong gust of wind caught
the sails and almost tipped us over. The storm
had come upon us so quickly that there had
been no time to lower the sails.

209

Unless the sails were lowered
quickly, the ship would capsize, and
we would all drown. It was unsafe,
however, to clamber about in the
rigging in the midst of a storm. No
one dared go up there for fear of
falling into the sea—no one but me.
Up the mast I shinnied, as bold as
a monkey.

When the sails were lowered,
the ship was no longer unsteady
and water no longer seeped in.
Weary sailors furled the sails
and stowed them safely. We
all huddled below the deck.
"Thank goodness for one bold
sailor in the crew!" they said—
meaning me!

Finally, the sun came out and the winds became calm. It was then that the captain sent for me.

The captain of our ship was Columbus himself. He put one arm around me and swept the other arm to the west. "Look!" he said to me. "Land! Yonder lies our safe harbor. When we drop anchor and go ashore, I will repay you properly. Until then, though, please accept the deepest thanks of your captain and shipmates. You have saved our lives."

My shipmates cheered, and I was a sailor at last.

Think About It

1. How does Manolo Sánchez become a real sailor?

2. After Manolo saves the ship, do you think the sailors feel bad that they had teased him? Why or why not?

3. On the day Manolo saves the ship, his father writes in his diary. He describes what happened and how he felt. Write the diary entry.

He Wrapped a Banana Around His Head

Oops! That title should be "He Wrapped a *Bandana* Around His Head." A mistake like that, confusing a word with one that sounds similar, is called a *malapropism*. It was named after Mrs. Malaprop, a character in a play from 1775. Her name, in turn, came from a French phrase meaning "not fitting the purpose." You may have unknowingly committed some malapropisms yourself!

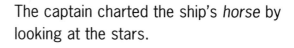

Columbus's voyage began a chain of events that led to a war called the American *Recollection*.

Sometimes sailors caught tropical *disguises* and felt unwell.

The sailors got hungry and discouraged when they ran low on *revisions*.

Crew members got up at the *croak* of dawn to return to their duties.

The captain charted the ship's *horse* by looking at the stars.

Consolations like the Big Dipper would reappear dependably every night.

If Columbus had never sailed, the history of the Western *Atmosphere* would be different.

213

THE MYSTERY GUEST

by KAYE GAGER

Time: *1850*
Place: *The Motts's Pennsylvania home*

CHARACTERS

Lucretia Mott,
*leader for women's rights
and freedom for slaves*

James Mott,
Lucretia's husband

Beth,
Lucretia's 11-year-old niece

Harriet Tubman, *leader
of the Underground Railroad*

Three or four escaped slaves

215

James Mott

Lucretia and her husband are seated at the kitchen table, talking quietly. Lucretia's niece, Beth, is doing needlework and listening outside the open door.

JAMES MOTT *(in a low voice)*: My dear, we have already been criticized for our views on women's suffrage. We will have to be very careful in the accomplishment of this new effort. If there is any suspicion of what we are up to here, our lives will assuredly be threatened!

LUCRETIA MOTT: I know it well, James. We've done everything we can to make our home safe for our guest. We cannot guarantee our own safety, but we will know we are doing the right thing.

JAMES: Assuredly, we are doing what any just interpreter of our acts would admit to be right. Tonight we must . . . What is that?! *(BETH has dropped her needlework. She steps out from behind the door.)*

Lucretia Mott

BETH: Is something wrong, Aunt Lucretia?

LUCRETIA: No, no, my dear. It's nothing that concerns you.

BETH: Are we having a guest? Who? Why didn't you tell me?

LUCRETIA (*hesitates*)**:** We are having a guest, but her identity must be kept secret. Let's just call her a mystery guest.

JAMES: Lucretia, we can't allow Beth to become involved. The risk is too great!

LUCRETIA: She already is involved, James. It's better that she should know a little of this matter. (*She turns to BETH.*) Our visitor will be coming quite late tonight, after you're in bed.

BETH: Should I get a room ready so she will be comfortable?

JAMES: I will get the cellar ready now. I must be emphatic, Lucretia—do not be careless and say too much. (*He leaves the room.*)

LUCRETIA: Come, Beth, you can help me get dinner ready. (*She moves toward stove and starts cooking.*)

BETH: Aunt Lucretia, why would the mystery guest stay in the cellar? Wouldn't the guest room be more suitable? Why won't you tell me who she is? Is she a celebrity?

LUCRETIA: To call her a celebrity would be misleading, though she is well known. Believe me, my dear, it is best for everyone that we keep our guest's identity a secret. Would you make yourself useful and hand me those napkins? (*BETH hands the napkins to LUCRETIA, who begins to make food bundles.*)

BETH: Why are we putting the food in napkins? We have plenty of plates.

LUCRETIA: Questions, questions! Don't worry, Beth, this is just what our guest will want.

(LUCRETIA and BETH put several bundles together.)

LUCRETIA *(looking out the window)*: It's nearly dark outside. I'm indebted to you, Beth, for your help. Now we're going to take these bundles out and set them on the stumps by the woodshed. *(BETH picks up a lantern.)* No! Don't take a light. We can see well enough without it.

BETH: How very strange! What kind of person could this mystery guest be? *(BETH and LUCRETIA leave the house.)*

(JAMES comes quietly out of the cellar.)

JAMES *(whispers)*: Everything is ready below. Let's get back inside. *(He quickly leads the way to the house.)*

Harriet Tubman

LUCRETIA: Now it's time for you to go to bed, Beth.

BETH: Aunt Lucretia! It's too early! I want to meet the mystery guest, too. Please!

LUCRETIA: Beth, I must be emphatic. It's better that you never meet this guest. Someday I will tell you all about her, but not now. Go, child. (*BETH heads slowly upstairs.*)

(*Later that night. LUCRETIA and JAMES are outside. Beth has slipped out and is hiding nearby to watch. Suddenly, HARRIET TUBMAN comes through the bushes. A small group of escaped slaves is behind her.*)

LUCRETIA (*whispering*): Welcome, distinguished guest. We respect you for your many accomplishments. Your work is a gift to humanity. We are grateful for it.

HARRIET TUBMAN: Thank you. I am indebted to you for your kindness. Without thoughtful folks like you, there would be no Underground Railroad.

(*The group joins hands and very softly sings the anthem "Free at Last," while Beth, in her hiding place, whispers along.*)

Think About It

1. Who is the mystery guest? Why is she going to stay in the cellar?

2. Why do you think Beth slips out of the house? How do you think she feels when she sees the mystery guest?

3. What do you think happens the next morning? Write the next part of the play.

Several routes of the Underground Railroad passing through New England

Who Was Poor Richard?

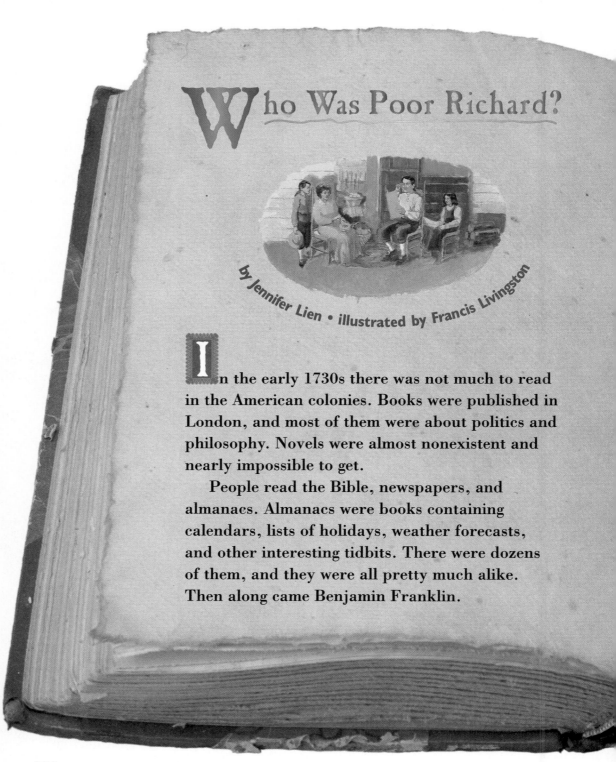

by Jennifer Lien • illustrated by Francis Livingston

In the early 1730s there was not much to read in the American colonies. Books were published in London, and most of them were about politics and philosophy. Novels were almost nonexistent and nearly impossible to get.

People read the Bible, newspapers, and almanacs. Almanacs were books containing calendars, lists of holidays, weather forecasts, and other interesting tidbits. There were dozens of them, and they were all pretty much alike. Then along came Benjamin Franklin.

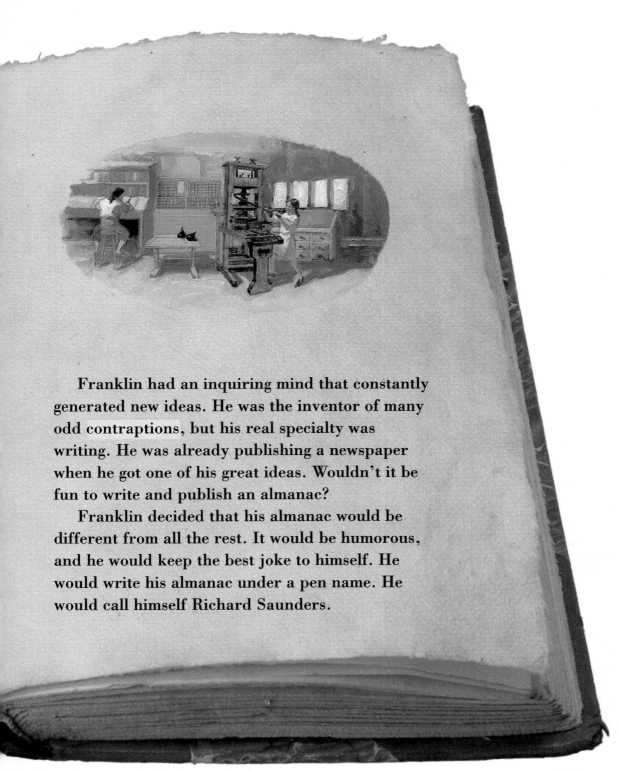

Franklin had an inquiring mind that constantly generated new ideas. He was the inventor of many odd contraptions, but his real specialty was writing. He was already publishing a newspaper when he got one of his great ideas. Wouldn't it be fun to write and publish an almanac?

Franklin decided that his almanac would be different from all the rest. It would be humorous, and he would keep the best joke to himself. He would write his almanac under a pen name. He would call himself Richard Saunders.

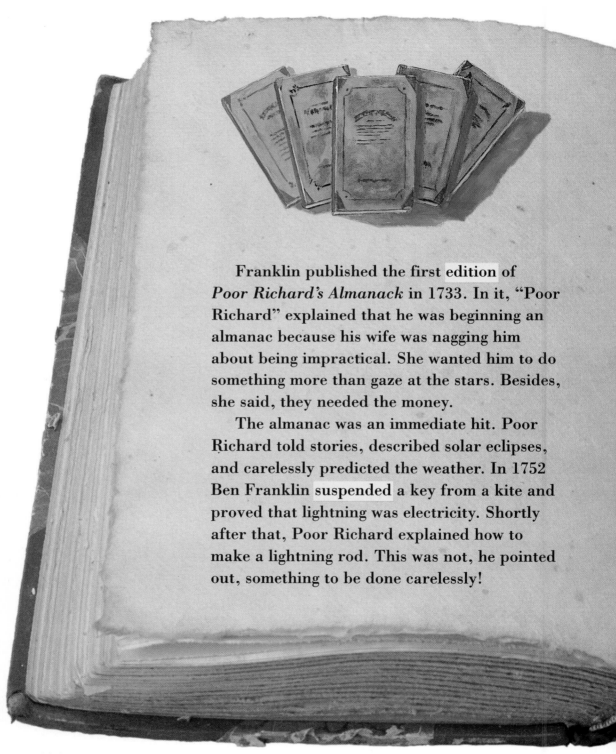

Franklin published the first edition of *Poor Richard's Almanack* in 1733. In it, "Poor Richard" explained that he was beginning an almanac because his wife was nagging him about being impractical. She wanted him to do something more than gaze at the stars. Besides, she said, they needed the money.

The almanac was an immediate hit. Poor Richard told stories, described solar eclipses, and carelessly predicted the weather. In 1752 Ben Franklin suspended a key from a kite and proved that lightning was electricity. Shortly after that, Poor Richard explained how to make a lightning rod. This was not, he pointed out, something to be done carelessly!

The almanac became known for something else. Poor Richard's new specialty was writing proverbs. His way of giving advice through short, humorous sayings brought nods and smiles from those who read them.

Here are a few that he published:

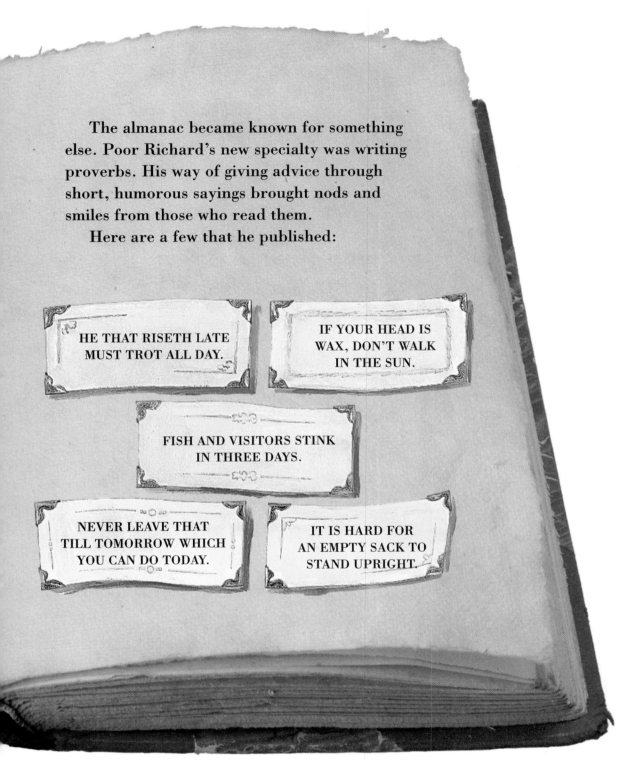

HE THAT RISETH LATE
MUST TROT ALL DAY.

IF YOUR HEAD IS
WAX, DON'T WALK
IN THE SUN.

FISH AND VISITORS STINK
IN THREE DAYS.

NEVER LEAVE THAT
TILL TOMORROW WHICH
YOU CAN DO TODAY.

IT IS HARD FOR
AN EMPTY SACK TO
STAND UPRIGHT.

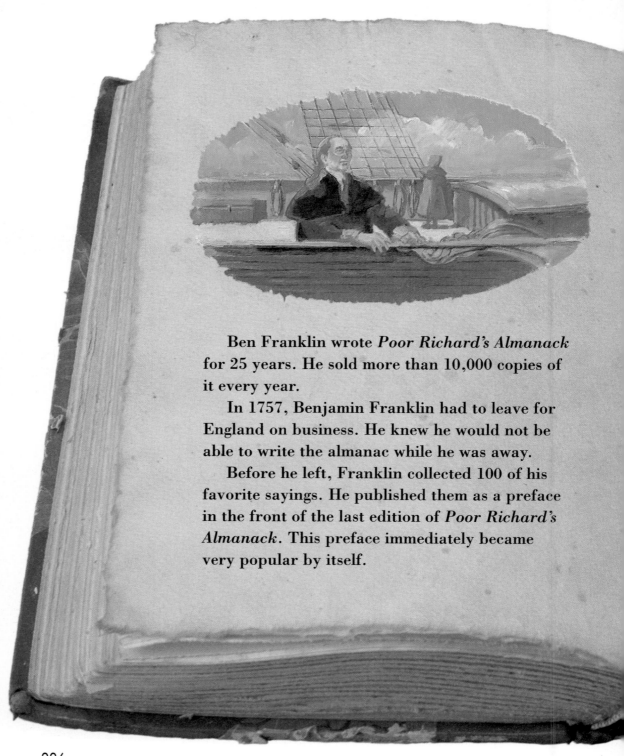

Ben Franklin wrote *Poor Richard's Almanack* for 25 years. He sold more than 10,000 copies of it every year.

In 1757, Benjamin Franklin had to leave for England on business. He knew he would not be able to write the almanac while he was away.

Before he left, Franklin collected 100 of his favorite sayings. He published them as a preface in the front of the last edition of *Poor Richard's Almanack*. This preface immediately became very popular by itself.

During his long life, Benjamin Franklin won many honors. In addition to being a writer and an inventor, he was a very skilled diplomat. He worked on many important matters. He got the British to repeal some of their taxes on the colonies. He helped draft the Declaration of Independence, too. (Some people were afraid to let him write it for fear he might conceal a joke in it!) After the colonies won their independence from England, Benjamin Franklin helped write the peace treaty.

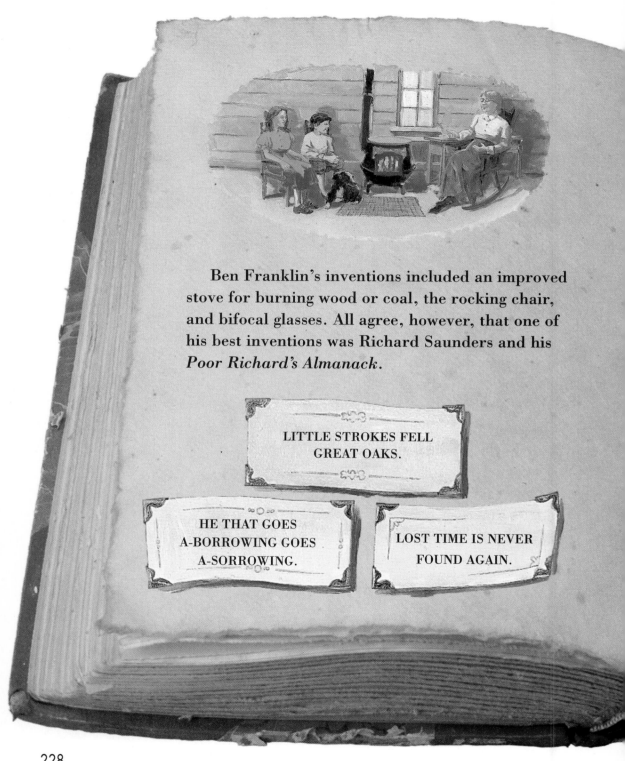

Ben Franklin's inventions included an improved stove for burning wood or coal, the rocking chair, and bifocal glasses. All agree, however, that one of his best inventions was Richard Saunders and his *Poor Richard's Almanack.*

LITTLE STROKES FELL
GREAT OAKS.

HE THAT GOES
A-BORROWING GOES
A-SORROWING.

LOST TIME IS NEVER
FOUND AGAIN.

Think About It

1. Who was Poor Richard? What did he do?

2. Why do you think Franklin chose to give advice in short, humorous sayings?

3. A newspaper might have printed an article about the last edition of *Poor Richard's Almanack*. Write a story that a newspaper could have printed.

The MISSION of the PONY EXPRESS

by Ben Farrell • illustrated by Lisa Carlson

Expeditions of explorers reached California long ago and described its beauty. Later, in 1849, it wasn't the land's beauty that made people rush west. It was the discovery of gold!

Most people didn't get rich in the California Gold Rush, but many decided to settle there anyway. Of course these settlers wanted to be able to get news and mail from back east.

At the time, news and mail moved west by train to Missouri. From there, it was transported to California by stagecoach. The distance was great and the terrain was rough. There were many perils along the trail.

Carrying the mail by stagecoach was a dismal ordeal that took weeks. A faster way to cover the distance from the riverbank of the Missouri to California was urgently needed. Meeting this need became the mission of the pony express.

The way the pony express worked was simple. A rider on horseback carried the mail at top speed from station to station along the route. At each station he mounted a fresh horse. After about 75 miles, another rider took over. Since riders traveled day and night, the mail reached California much faster than it did by stagecoach.

The pony express needed many people besides these relay riders. Station workers were also hired to take care of the horses and feed the riders.

The job held in highest esteem was that of rider. Ads called for young men under eighteen willing to risk their lives every day. Riders needed to be brave to face the perils they would encounter in this job.

The boys who came to the riverbank office of the pony express knew the dangers they might encounter— wild animals or mail robbers. Still, they couldn't pass up the promise of good pay.

The first pony express rider left St. Joseph, Missouri, in April 1860. He may have been pelted by heavy rain, but he kept going. The riders who crossed the mountains may have been blinded by snow. They, too, kept riding.

Ten days later, his mission completed, the last relay rider galloped into Sacramento, California. Bands played, and a cheering crowd thanked him profusely. The mail and news had arrived faster than ever before, thanks to the pony express!

The pony express carried news and mail for just 19 months. In 1861, telegraph lines finally reached California, connecting the west coast to the east. The invention of the telegraph in 1837 had provided a faster way to send news. Not long after that, the railroads were extended across the country. They provided a faster way to send mail.

Though the pony express didn't last long, it is an exciting part of our history. Some of its riders gained fame after their time in the pony express.

One such rider was William F. Cody. He was just
fourteen when he went to work for the pony express. His
job at first was to ride 45 miles and reach the next rider
in three hours. Older or more experienced riders had to
cover a greater distance.

Later in his life, William Cody told stories of his days
with the pony express. Once he had to ride 384 miles
without rest! Cody also gained fame as a hunter, scout,
cowboy, and showman. People who visited his Wild West
Show knew him as Buffalo Bill Cody. The pony express
action story he put into his show thrilled audiences all
over the world.

Think About It

1. What did pony express riders do? Why did this job take a lot of courage?

2. How do you think pony express riders felt about their work?

3. You are a pony express rider and have just completed your first ride. Write a letter home telling about your ride.

Frontier

by Kana Riley

In the predawn light, the sea of grass ripples in unending waves across the plains. The rising sun wakes the children, and they crawl out from under their comfortable quilts. It is time to do the chores.

At first the children yawn and blink sleepily. Outside their sod home, however, their energy is restored by the fresh air, and they shiver in the early morning chill. Fall comes early in this climate, and soon the grass will be covered with snow.

Children

The girl grabs a milk pail and a three-legged stool. Her designated chore is to milk the cow that waits in the small barn. Like the house, the barn is made of chunks of sod cut from the grassland.

The girl's younger brother tosses handfuls of corn to the chickens and then feeds the mule. The hungry animals crowd around him trustingly.

Both children work quickly because today is a school day, and they don't want to be late. They will be sorry when snow makes it impossible to get to the schoolhouse. Then they will have to stay home.

Children living on farms today are still expected to be capable helpers.

239

The climate of the plains is often harsh. In winter the snow-covered plains can seem empty and desolate.

This will be the family's second winter on the plains. Two summers ago they crossed the country in a wagon train as part of the great exodus from the East. Hundreds of families migrated to the West to find good farming land.

When they got to their land, it seemed to the children a useless and desolate place—not a single tree grew anywhere. Their father had dug a hole into the side of a hill, the way a burrowing animal does. He had walled up the open

side, and that's where they had spent the first winter.

Their home back East had been in a town. The children thought they would dislike homesteading in a community where friends and farms were miles apart.

Finally spring came, and the family set to work to construct a proper house. In other parts of the frontier, people lived in adobe houses or log cabins. On the plains, there was no clay for making adobe bricks, and there were no trees to provide logs for a cabin. The new home would be a "soddy," built of bricks cut from the sod.

As soon as the sod home was finished, the family turned to planting crops. The parents plowed the land, and the children planted seeds and hauled water.

In the fall the whole family harvested the crops. They put some foods aside for winter and sold the rest in town. They earned enough money to pay the first installment on the loan they had taken for the land.

Some farmers still use horse-drawn plows to cut through sod.

"Breakfast!" the children's mother calls. This morning it's homemade bread and jam. The girl smiles, remembering the pailful of berries she collected to make the jam.

Their mother puts a hard-boiled egg in each of their lunch pails. "Fresh from your chickens," the boy's father says to him with a smile.

The girl helps her brother onto the mule and climbs up behind him. Riding to school is certainly better than walking!

At the schoolhouse, children are playing Snap-the-Whip before school begins. They have formed a long line, holding hands. The leader pulls the line in fast turns, trying to make those on the end lose their grip.

The girl and boy join in the friendly game. They are no longer unhappy here. Running and shouting with their new friends, they forget how desolate this homesteading community once seemed to them. Now it is home.

One teacher taught children of all ages who attended this one-room sod schoolhouse.

Think About It

1. How is the family's frontier house different from their old house?

2. How do you think the girl and boy feel about doing their chores?

3. The girl sends a letter to a friend back in the town her family left. She tells her friend about her new life on the plains. Write the letter the girl sends.

Mule Rules

Here's a silly verse. If you know the tune of "Auld Lang Syne," you can sing along.

On mules we find
two legs behind
and two we find before.

We stand behind
before we find
what the two behind be for.

When we're behind
the two behind,
we find what they be for.

So stand before
the two behind,
behind the two before!